OWN
YOUR
WEIRD

AN ODDLY EFFECTIVE WAY FOR FINDING
HAPPINESS IN WORK, LIFE, AND LOVE

JASON ZOOK

RUNNING PRESS
PHILADELPHIA

Running Press
Hachette Book Group
1290 Avenue of the Americas, New York, NY 10104
www.runningpress.com
@Running_Press

Printed in the United States of America

Published by Running Press, an imprint of Perseus Books, LLC,
a subsidiary of Hachette Book Group, Inc. The Running Press name
and logo is a trademark of the Hachette Book Group.

The Hachette Speakers Bureau provides a wide range of authors for speaking events.
To find out more, go to www.hachettespeakersbureau.com or call (866) 376-6591.

The publisher is not responsible for websites (or their content) that are not owned by the publisher.

Cover photo copyright © by Getty Images/ Matjaz Slanic & Vudhikul Ocharoen
Print book cover and interior design by Joshua McDonnell

Library of Congress Control Number: Library of Congress Cataloging-in-Publication Data
has been applied for.

ISBNs: 978-0-7624-6717-4 (hardcover) 978-0-7624-6716-7 (ebook)

LSC-C

10   9   8   7   6   5   4   3   2   1

CONTENTS

INTRODUCTION

The way things have always been done is NOT the way things have to be done. It's time to own your weird.

As I sat in the courtroom, looking around at people who were also sitting with their lawyers, waiting to get some sort of approval from that day's appointed judge, it slapped me in the face just how much I own my weird.

Was I sitting in the courtroom because I'd committed a nefarious crime? Was I uncomfortably squirming in the wooden pew next to my lawyer because of some crazy offshore banking embezzlement scheme gone wrong? Was I there like most other folks who were going through a divorce or child custody battle? No friend, alas, I was there for a much more unique reason: I had sold my last name (via an online auction) and was trying to legally change my name from Jason Sadler to Jason Headsetsdotcom. Yep.

After what seemed like hours of waiting, my case number was finally called. I "approached the bench" (my Judge Judy moment!) and the judge reviewed my case file. I remember him looking at my file very differently than he had the twenty or so cases before me. As he read the official paperwork his head cocked slightly like a dog when you make a high-pitched whistling sound. He then proceeded to ask a bunch of questions like, "Have you been convicted of any felonies recently?" and "Are you trying to avoid creditors by changing your last name?" and the final one, "What exactly does the name 'Headsetsdotcom' mean?" It was clearly a resounding "NO" to the first two questions, but for some reason I was nervous and barely squeaked out my reply. Luckily my lawyer handled the explanation of the new last name because he could tell I was in full flop-sweat and could barely form sentences.

Then, and I kid you not, with a swing of his actual wooden gavel, he stated, "I've never had a name change request like this, here we go" and my legal last name was changed. It had to be the weirdest case he made a decision on that day/week/month.

To get you caught up on how this story started, a few months prior I'd found out my parents were getting a divorce and the name I'd used for most of my life (Sadler) was now completely meaningless to me. To make things more interesting, it was my third last name by age thirty and I was now left with an odd predicament. What do you do when you have a last name you no longer want? No stranger to putting myself out there and doing unconventional things, as we'll get to later in the book, I decided instead of leafing through the White Pages to attempt to discover a last name I liked, I'd create an online auction to the legal rights of my last name for a year. Think of it like an eBay auction, but instead of bidding on some electronic gadget, you'd be bidding for the ability to change my last name to your company's name.

Within twenty-four hours of launching the aptly named website BuyMyLastName.com in 2012, the auction to own the rights to my last name went from $0 and skyrocketed to $33,333. That is not a typo, that was an actual thing that happened! The bidding didn't stop there and after thirty days my last name was purchased by the headsets company Headsets.com for $45,500. My full name would be Jason Headsetsdotcom and with the visit to the courthouse and subsequent visit to the DMV, my driver's license told the entire (weird) story.

You may have picked up this book because you're the type of person who knows you're a little weird (or wants to stop fitting in and start owning your weird) but is nervous about the unknowns that come along with that. Will embracing your weird still allow you to have a job that provides the money you and your family need? If you commit to being truly your weird self, will you feel fulfilled in how you spend your time on a daily/weekly/monthly/yearly basis? I'm (weird) living proof there's another option to what the majority of society tells you is the "right" way to live and work. I didn't know that I'd be able to carve out my own path when I was young, but I remember a constant nagging thought that there had to be another way to live, work, and succeed as an adult. A way that felt more akin to me and who I was as a person. A way where I could own my weird.

I think back to my childhood often, remembering the burning desire to accept who I was as a weird person and to not accept life as it was force-fed to me. With this came the constant thought: *Why do I need to do X like other people? Why can't I do things my own unique way?*

These days I don't even think about owning my weird anymore—it's completely automatic. I've come to understand that I'm wired differently. This instinctive impulse I have to question convention, embrace what sets me apart, and avoid following in someone else's footsteps has ultimately translated into a business and life that I absolutely love.

Avoiding the well-traveled paths that others have laid out (what I like to call "The Sea of Sameness") in order to forge my own has not only allowed me to stand out as an entrepreneur (leading to profitable businesses and an engaged audience), but it has also led me to design a life that's built around who I am as a person, with my unique values and what makes me happy.

It turns out the recipe for success and happiness is in the realization that there is no recipe—you have to own your weird and carve out your own path toward happiness, success, and fulfillment.

The good news is that you don't actually need special DNA to own your weird, you already have it! You simply need to develop a mindset that challenges societal norms and embraces your own uniqueness. But how do you do that? Well, that's what I want to share with you in this book.

BREAKING AWAY FROM BEIGE

In 2005, a young guy from England by the name of Alex Tew had an idea to help him pay for university that he simply named The Million Dollar Homepage. On this homepage that he created, there were a million pixels available for purchase. Each pixel was $1, and anyone could purchase these pixels to advertise whatever they wanted. Pretty freakin' weird idea, huh?

The moment I came across Alex's inspiring and creative project, it actually blew my mind. This was partially due to the fact that, at that moment, I was living the opposite of an inspiring and creative life. I was living a completely beige existence at a 9-to-5 job as a graphic designer. Everything was literally (and metaphorically) beige, from the chair I sat in, to the desk I worked at, to the walls I stared at, down to the squeaky drawers that held my files. Even the monitor that I pushed (non-million-dollar) pixels around on was beige. So when The Million Dollar Homepage landed in my inbox from a co-worker, it truly was like an explosion of color and creativity slapping me in the face.

I thought to myself: *You can DO something like this?*

The stark contrast between the bland job I was seeing in front of me and that stubborn kid that wanted to do everything his own way was suddenly so obvious. Somehow I'd slowly drifted away from that essential part of me that was always asking *Why does it have to be this way?* and I'd just accepted what I thought I was supposed to want (a good job, owning a house, a fancy car, etc.). The Million Dollar Homepage was the jolt of inspiration I needed to start seeing my beige world for exactly what it was: a boring, cookie-cutter path. The opposite of what I really wanted.

This realization planted a seed that would later turn into several of my own *"you can do something like this?"* ideas, but it all began because I finally started waking up to the fact that the path I was on wasn't what I wanted for my life. I realized that owning my weird ideas and unique personality traits would actually help me stand out and get noticed.

Maybe you, too, have your own version of that beige existence right now—something that feels like it doesn't quite fit. An element of your life that you've chosen because you think you should, not because it's what you really want (or a reflection of who you truly are at your core). Acknowledging the *beigeness* is the first step toward a whole new way of seeing the world, which is exactly what I'm hoping to show you in the pages of this book.

WHY I WROTE THIS BOOK

When I finished writing my first book, *Creativity for Sale*, it was 2013 and I was in the middle of a huge transition. I had just learned a ton (especially during the writing of the book) about how some aspects of being an entrepreneur had caused me to focus my attention on the wrong things in my life. I was starting to learn that subscribing to the "hustle" mentality—always chasing down external validation (more work, more press, more customers, more money, more social media followers)—wasn't what would ultimately lead me to happiness.

I can honestly say the experience of writing *Creativity for Sale* was pivotal to understanding myself better, and that deeper understanding became a catalyst for some big changes in my thinking and my lifestyle over the years that followed.

I decided to dust off the old typewriter (okay fine, MacBook Pro, but what if I did write this whole thing on a dusty typewriter?) and write this book as a "second installment" of sorts because I want to share those shifts in perspective with you. The five years between writing *Creativity for Sale* and the book you hold in your hands taught me some big lessons—lessons that will hopefully provide you with an alternative to some of the more traditional ways of living and running a business.

I also chose to write this book because I've finally reached a point in my life where I know how important owning my weird is to my personal sense of fulfillment. It feels completely tied to who I am on a cellular level. Every idea, project, or business has to be weird or unique in some way. If I had to boil my personality down to one single thing, it would be my inability to accept the established or predictable route in anything. Like a person who has to straighten every pen on their desk to sit at a perfect 45-degree angle (no, I don't actually do that!), I get physically uncomfortable when I do things the same way other people do them. This personal discovery feels like the one thing I'm actually qualified to write a book on (not that being qualified has ever stopped me from doing anything in the past!) and the one message I feel most excited to share with the world at this stage of my life.

IT'S ABOUT YOU

....

In this book, you're going to read a lot of stories about how the idea of owning your weird shows up in my life and my business. But you don't have to be like me (or like Mike) in order to find value in straying from the herd. The stories may be about me, but this book isn't really about me; it's about you.

Why is the idea of owning your weird valuable to YOU?

Well, if one of your reasons for picking up this book was to have a more profitable business, owning your weird (a.k.a. standing out from the crowd) is pretty much Marketing 101. Yet so many entrepreneurs and creative business owners I know keep trying to follow the road map laid out by that blog post or podcast episode or that thing a "thought leader" said at a conference they went to.

This book is about you realizing that the blueprint does not exist—not if you want to actually stand out in your field. You are going to have to ignore the norm, take a risk, and go all in on what makes you different from everyone else. All of my biggest business successes have come from doubling down on my difference. From being willing to let my "freak flag fly." From listening to the nagging voice in my head that says "myyyy preciouuusssss . . . " Oh wait, that's not me . . . From listening to the voice in my head that constantly pushes me to think way outside the box and own my weird. If you, too, have that nagging voice, I want this book to remind you to give owning your weird a chance. And if you don't, I want this book to teach you how to get it to speak up.

Believe me when I say that owning your weird will not only help you get the attention you're seeking (the first step to getting more customers is awareness), but it will also help you run a business that feels authentic to who you actually are.

That brings me to the more important reason learning to own your weird is valuable: **your life is bigger than your business.** It matters what you spend your time and energy on. It matters whether you're making decisions based on what other people want for you and what society expects of you or if you're choosing what *you* want deep down.

If there's one thing I want you to take away from this book it's that you can rewrite the rules to whatever part of your life you want. **The way things have always been done is NOT the way things have to be done.** But, it starts with you. You have to decide that you won't accept things as they've been presented to you—that there's more than just beige out there, and you're willing to take the risk to go find it for yourself.

OWNING YOUR WEIRD ISN'T EASY

I'm not going to sugarcoat it for you, though: Owning your weird is hard. Going against the grain pretty much guarantees that you'll encounter rejection and ridicule and uncertainty and failure (and yes, I get into all of that in this book, too. I'm not about to skate over the hard stuff). It's challenging to step outside that damn proverbial box everyone talks about. But what I've found, and what I want to share with you throughout this book, is that **even though owning your weird can be challenging, it's also the most rewarding feeling to embrace who you are and what makes you unique.**

I've experienced success (as most people would define it) in two different ways: (1) following the paths laid out by other people, and (2) carving out my own, slightly more curved, rocky, and where-the-heck-do-I-take-my-next-step path. While growing a business based on the proven tactics and strategies of other people is by no means a bad idea (there's plenty we can learn from people who are already winning), I've found that achieving success using someone else's recipe and ignoring your weird often leaves you feeling empty. Why? Because how you feel when you get to that next level depends, in part, on how you feel about *how* you got there.

When you reach some level of success and achieve something you set out to do, there are two types of mental rewards that happen. The first is based on the outcome of your efforts—the feeling of accomplishment that comes with completing a goal (selling your art, landing more clients, having a big product launch, etc). When you get what you had your eye on, it feels great! That's the first mental reward.

The second comes from *how* you achieved that outcome. When you've hacked down your own weird path, it means you've navigated the inevitable challenges and roadblocks and managed to come through it victorious (with the scars to prove it). There's an extra sense of satisfaction deep down in your gut knowing *you* did the work necessary and you pioneered new territory for yourself. That second mental reward gives you all the right feels, and it makes the first reward that much sweeter. Going your own weird way may be harder, but success that feels authentically earned is far more fulfilling.

HOW THIS BOOK IS STRUCTURED

I decided to organize this book into three main sections: (1) the core tenets of adopting an **Own Your Weird** mindset; (2) how I've applied those tenets in various parts of my life and business over the past five years; and (3) practical advice for how you can take these ideas forward and create your own custom blueprint for success, in your own way.

SECTION I: THE OWN YOUR WEIRD MINDSET

As I mentioned, I want this book to be about you more than it is about me. That's why the first section is full of six important lessons I've uncovered the past few years—lessons that can be applied to your life and business immediately. Together they make up what I refer to as the "Own Your Weird mindset," which can serve as a powerful tool for navigating the world on your own terms.

SECTION II: HOW I OWN MY WEIRD

Once you know the core parts of the Own Your Weird mindset, I want to share with you several ways in which I've applied this mindset to various aspects of my own life the past few years. My hope is that by seeing how I have forged my own path in everything from health to marriage to business, you might be able to see how these principles can apply uniquely to various aspects of your own life.

SECTION III: CREATING YOUR OWN YOUR WEIRD BLUEPRINT IN BUSINESS AND LIFE

In this final section, we'll talk about ways that you can put these principles and my examples together to write your own blueprint. As you already know, one of the core themes of this book is about letting go of the idea that there is any single path or blueprint you can follow out there and learning to just carve out your own as you go. In this section, I share with you some final thoughts about how to do just that.

IS THIS A BUSINESS BOOK?

You might be thinking to yourself, wait a second, Jason, isn't this supposed to be a business book? Isn't business what you normally write about? So far it sounds like a book about life. Or, dare I say it, a . . . *personal development* book (*shudder*).

Business book, life book, memoir, self-help book . . . Hell if I know. If it's hard to tell at times where this book fits in, it's because life and business go hand-in-hand for me. They're virtually one and the same. We'll dig into this work/life blend later in the book, but for now just prepare yourself for a wide range of topics throughout these pages, covering everything from Facebook ads for business to eating a vegan diet. I may jump around a lot, but every topic, every tangent, every word is in service of the idea that owning your weird is your key to getting what you want out of your one, precious life.

You might also notice I haven't loaded up this book with tons of carefully researched examples of other people and businesses owning their weird. I know that tends to be the formula for these kind of "prove your thesis" books, but honestly I don't love those kinds of books. (Plus, as you can tell already, if there's a "formula" for something, I don't want any part of it.) What you're about to read is almost entirely my experiences, my opinions, and my perspective. I hope you're cool with that.

THE QUICK JASON ZOOK RECAP:
MY JOURNEY THROUGH
OWN-YOUR-WEIRD-LAND

All right, now that we're on the same page with the why and the how and the what and all that jazz, the next order of business is to catch you up on a few topics that you'll hear me reference throughout this book. I went into much more detail about most of these things in my first self-published book *Creativity for Sale*, but I realize you may not have read it. If you did, thank you, but it was probably light-years ago. If you didn't, don't worry, this is one of those stand-alone sequels that doesn't require you to know all the backstory. As far as book sequels go, it's like the *Fast & Furious: Tokyo Drift* of follow-up books (without the bad writing or Lil Bow Wow's atrocious green car).

If you *are* the type that likes to know ALL the things and get up to speed (like my wife, Caroline, who reads the IMDB synopsis *before* going into a movie), I've included a little "Jason Zook Recap" of sorts that will catch you up on the major milestones and primary characters from *Creativity for Sale* (and beyond) that I'll be referencing in this book.

IWEARYOURSHIRT (2008-2013)

Remember when I told you about *The Million Dollar Homepage* and I said I came up with a few of my own *"You can do that?"* ideas . . . well, the first of those ideas was a business I started called IWearYourShirt. Almost every lesson I've learned in business has come from the five years I got paid to wear sponsored T-shirts for a living. And yes, that's exactly what IWearYourShirt was: a social media marketing company (before anyone knew what social media really was or how to use it) where businesses hired me to wear their logos on my T-shirt each day and create branded content for them on Facebook, YouTube, and Twitter. On a "normal" day I planned to take a photo in the shirt, which got posted to all my social network profiles. Then I'd film, edit, and upload a YouTube video where I tried to do something fun or entertaining in the shirt. Last but not least I also hosted a one-hour live video show where I interacted with complete strangers from around the world who, for some reason that still eludes me to this day, wanted to watch a random dude wear a shirt and sit on a couch.

IWearYourShirt launched in October 2008, and I wore my first sponsored T-shirt on January 1, 2009 for a paltry $1. That's not a typo (my copyeditor asked multiple times, too). The pricing structure for IWearYourShirt was to sell daily sponsorships at face value according to the day of the year. Being that January 1 is the first day of the year, that day cost $1. Then the price increased by $1 per day, so January 2 was $2, January 3 was $3, and so on, all the way until December 31, which sold for $365. This pricing would become known as "bumpsale" pricing (and I even created a simple software product with my good friend Conrad many years later so other people could do "bumpsales" of their own.)

In 2009, it was just me wearing daily sponsored T-shirts and promoting the company of the day through social media updates on Facebook and Twitter; one daily, hour-long live video show on Ustream; as well as an edited YouTube video focused on the daily sponsor. I created this mix of daily content for each of the 365 days in 2009, including every weekend and major holiday. (Crazy, huh?)

In 2010, I grew the business to two T-shirt wearers—myself and a guy named Evan White in California—and doubled the price ($2 per day increasing). Then, in 2011, I grew it to five shirt wearers with the same sponsor, and in 2012, five shirt wearers all with different individual sponsors. By that time, the business had started to fail. There are too many reasons for that to share here—and you can read about all of them in my first book, *Creativity for Sale* (sales pitch, heyo!)—but the point is that IWearYourShirt finally closed its doors on May 6, 2013 when I officially announced my retirement from professional T-shirt wearing. I believe the Pope himself cried when he heard the news of my retirement. Or I completely made that up in my mind? Probably the latter.

While the ending of IWearYourShirt was not what I'd ever hoped for, the business did generate more than $1 million in total revenue when it was active, and as I mentioned, it taught me almost everything I know about business, sales, and marketing.

It's important to note that even though the business generated more than $1 million in its life span, I didn't walk away with all that money. Quite the opposite, in fact. By the time I shut the business down, I ended up over $100,000 in debt.

But, don't cry for me, Argentina! I've since paid off all that debt and I go into detail about how I did it later on in this very book you're holding.

BUYMYLASTNAME (2012–2014)

In the opening paragraphs of this book you were introduced to this crazy project that popped into my brain. I auctioned off the rights to change my last name to the highest bidder—and I did it twice! This idea came to me after a family divorce left me with a last name I no longer wanted, my third last name in my lifetime. I was already a walking billboard . . . why not use my last name as buyable ad space, too?

In November 2012, I started an auction at $0 and in the first twenty-four hours, the bidding to own my last name for one year was up to $33,333! Yep, I'm still as shocked as you are. The bidding ended at $45,500 and my legal last name for 2013 was Jason Headsetsdotcom. You may be wondering why the heck a company would buy someone's last name? Well, I'd built a sizeable audience on social media and knew a crazy idea like this would get attention, which all companies love and need to grow (and it did: my last name sale was featured on the homepage of *USA Today* and tons of prominent TV news outlets talked about it). Don't think for a moment I phoned this idea in either, as I mentioned earlier I even went to a courthouse and stood in front of a judge (twice!), asking for permission to legally change my name to such a silly thing. At the end of 2013, I decided to do this last name auction one last time, and the bidding for that one ended at $50,000. The rights to change my last name went to a surfing app (Surfr), and they named me Jason SurfrApp. Just like that, I'd made nearly $100,000 (10 percent of which was donated to charity) and I'd taken a negative family situation and turned into a money-making opportunity.

The name you see on the cover of this book, Jason Zook, is my final and forever name. Zook was my great-grandfather's last name, and I'm happy to carry his name and lineage forward, as he was also an entrepreneur. (Although, I'm guessing his business ideas weren't quite as weird as mine.)

SPONSORMYBOOK (2013)

You heard me mention my first book, *Creativity for Sale*. What I didn't mention was that (of course) I didn't want my first book to be published in any traditional or nonweird way. Many people told me that first-time authors, especially ones that self-publish, rarely make money on their first book. I wanted to challenge this assumption so I came up with an idea I called SponsorMyBook.

Taking a page from my IWearYourShirt days (get it, it's a book pun!), I decided to sell sponsorships at the bottom of all two hundred pages of the book. They were simple text-only 140-character messages that anyone could purchase and use to advertise their business or get any message out they wanted to. When it was all said and done, I had sold space on the bottom of every page (including the front and back covers, as well as the inside flaps) for a total revenue of $75,000. I made all of this ad revenue before I ever wrote a single word of the book. Not bad for a first-time author!

BUYMYFUTURE/BUYOURFUTURE (2015–2017)

The years following SponsorMyBook/*Creativity for Sale* for me were all about exploration, reinvention, and finding my identity separate from the "T-shirt guy" persona I'd known. I tried my hand at a lot of different things, including public speaking, online courses, and building software (more on that later.) I made and sold online courses, built software side projects, and started building an audience that was interested in my perspective on creative marketing and business. But after a few years, I started to feel that familiar itch of needing to go way outside the box again. I wasn't doing things weird enough and wasn't getting much personal satisfaction from my efforts.

That's when the idea struck me for BuyMyFuture. I had just finished making my morning coffee (hand-crafted via a Chemex) and I was sitting at my white IKEA desk staring out a floor-to-ceiling window. I had committed myself for a few weeks to a morning ritual of writing down ten random business ideas per day while drinking my coffee. As I sipped from my mug, scribbling down any idea that came to me, a little light bulb of a thought came soaring from the catacombs of my brain to whatever part of the front of your brain actually synthesizes thoughts into coherent ideas. It asked this question: *"What if I didn't sell all my stuff separately, what if I just sold one thing? And what if that one thing included all my future things?"*

These two simple questions led to a crazy weird idea: For one price, someone could purchase access to all my past projects (eight online courses, two books, and two software products) AND they'd also get **anything I ever created in the future at no additional cost.**

Essentially someone would be . . . wait for it . . . buying my future.

BuyMyFuture launched for the first time in September 2015 and was available for two weeks at $1,000. I had set a public goal of 100 purchases and was pleasantly surprised when BuyMyFuture sales closed at 178! One cup of coffee leading to $178,000 in revenue—that brew must have been strong!

After another successful launch (at a higher price of $1,500) in 2016, I knew I wanted to keep the idea fresh by adding a twist in 2017. My wife, Caroline (who is an artist and online course creator with her own business, Made Vibrant), and I started to notice that our audiences had a lot of overlap. She was running into the problem of having too many products to sell as well, so after a few long afternoon walk-and-talks with our dog Plaxico (an adorable Staffordshire Bull Terrier), we decided to turn BuyMyFuture into Buy*Our*Future. A potential buyer would get everything we'd *both* created and anything we *both* would ever create moving forward.

All-in, the BuyMyFuture/BuyOurFuture idea has brought in nearly $500,000 in revenue the past three years and I still consider it the most fun idea I've ever conceived. What started as a way for me to have to sell fewer things all the time, has turned into the best community I've ever been a part of and a monthly membership community that my wife and I run called Wandering Aimfully (the BuyOurFuture spots are now sold as monthly membership spots). There's not a day that goes by that I don't enjoy interacting with our BuyOurFuture/Wandering Aimfully community members (especially as they help and support one another with no prodding from us).

THIS BOOK! OWN YOUR WEIRD (2016–2018)

Speaking of books, I should probably catch you up on how this book came to be because it had quite a unique journey that's a major departure from how most books come to life.

In 2016 I decided I wanted to write my second book (two years after *Creativity for Sale*), but I knew I wanted to do something . . . weird. One evening in September 2016 at dinner I blurted something along the lines of: *What if I wrote my next book and let anyone around the world watch me type the words, real-time?* My wife, who was on the receiving end of the blurting, agreed that it was a bizarre but interesting idea, mostly from the perspective that authors hate showing the first drafts of their writing. Because I can never go half-assed with one of my ideas, I knew I wasn't going to use Google Docs and share a link for anyone to join, I had to make the experience feel bigger and create an environment that would be conducive to helping me get my book's first draft written. I sketched out in a notebook what I thought a live-writing environment would look like as a simple website and added a live chat element for people to interact while they watched my words appear on screen. With the help of a developer friend, the website WatchMeWrite.co was born and I was off to the writing races. I had a live editor application I could write in behind the scenes and anyone from around the world could log in during my daily writing hours (9 a.m.–1 p.m.). I wrote for fourteen days straight in December 2016 and even recorded a behind-the-scenes podcast at the same time to talk about the experience and continue to bring people along for the book-creation journey. There were also two awesome companies who sponsored the WatchMeWrite idea (Podia and Acuity Scheduling), and I received over $1,500 in donations from people who watched live as my awful first draft came to life (not too shabby!).

You may think the story ends there, but alas it does not. Once the first draft was finished I paid an editor to go through and clean things up. One thing I don't have any problem with is cranking out words and getting some writing done but I do struggle at weaving things together and that's why I knew having a structural editor help in the beginning would take my crappy writing and make it at least coherent. From there, Caroline took a pass at editing the book, and at that time I was full-steam ahead with the idea that I'd self-publish the book and move on to another project. But then another idea hit me: *What if I made a website that publicly asked a traditional book publisher or book agent to scoop up the rights to my second book. Wouldn't that be weird? Wouldn't that buck the conventional system of how books get published? Heck yeah it would!* I created and launched a second website for this book titled DearBookPublisher.com and announced that for one month I'd be open to talk to publishers or agents about traditionally bringing my second book to life (there was even a fancy promo video of me walking in slow motion at sunset with a mock-up copy of the book in hand, it was sex-ayyy!).

After a few weeks and a handful of emails, I had a call with a wonderful agent at a New York literary agency. She helped me take the DearBookPublisher.com website and turn it into a more standard book proposal (you know, a PDF) and worked her magic to land a call with an awesome acquisitions editor at Running Press, where it's now set to become one of the most unconventionally traditionally published books ever. I mean, it has to be one of the weirdest journeys of a book, right? This just goes to show you how far creativity and doing things your own way can take you!

CAROLINE ZOOK (2010–PRESENT)

I think it's worth mentioning that throughout this book, you'll read Caroline's name many times. We met via a Twitter Direct Message in 2010 (yes, SO romantic), when then–college student Caroline was president of University of Florida's Advertising Society and was looking for a speaker to Skype in to talk to her group. From our first messages and emails, I knew it was love at first sight and the rest was easy and like a dream come true . . . Ahhh, who am I kidding? We were both in other relationships at the time and it all kind of happened by accident (or by her careful plotting, we'll never know . . . that is until she writes her tell-all autobiography and I find out along with you!).

Caroline is an incredibly important person in my life, not just from the emotionally-connected-forever standpoint, but also as a creative thinker and business partner. She makes me laugh constantly. She laughs at (most of) my jokes. She pushes me to be a better person and accepts all three of my faults.

Caroline, if you're reading this, I'm telling the world I love you, but I also want them to know how much I respect your opinions, ideas, and the fact that you embrace all my crazy weirdness. I always rolled my eyes when people said they married their best friend, but I absolutely did that. Ugh, so cliché and ooey-gooey, I know. Just deal with it! . . . And, also understand how important Caroline has been to me since we met in that 140-character message on Twitter because she'll be popping up in these pages quite a bit.

✳✳✳

"Own it!"

(KEEP AN EYE OUT FOR THESE SECTION RECAPS AND ACTION ITEMS)

As a person who reads books myself, I love it when there are succinct takeaways that leave me feeling empowered and as though I've done what I'm supposed to do with the information I was just given. For you, dear reader, I've included section recaps called "Own it!" where I break down the singular task or weird next step you should take in your life.

When you get through a section of this book, find the "Own it!" task, complete it, and feel free to shout out loud "I OWNED IT!" Obviously it's best to do these "Own it!" tasks in public places where you can look up from your laptop and yell at the top of your lungs, completely confusing everyone around you. Doesn't that sound fun? Okay, fine. You don't have to yell "I OWNED IT" in public, but maybe give yourself a little fist pump and then keep getting things done.

SECTION I

THE OWN YOUR WEIRD MINDSET

CHAPTER 1

Embrace Your Weirdness

A few years ago, while I was still a bit lost and trying to discover what to do next after IWearYourShirt, I found myself taking on more speaking invitations to keep cash coming in while I figured things out.

It was 2015, and I remember standing in a large conference room in Pittsburgh, PA, where I had been asked to do a ten-minute TED-style talk. There would be four speakers giving back-to-back talks to an audience of nearly five hundred people. Now, any sane person would prepare a presentation for that, or at the VERY LEAST a basic topic idea for their talk. No one in their right mind would stand stage left thinking to themselves, "Hmmm . . . I wonder what I should talk to this large audience of people about?" But that's exactly what I did.

As I stood there in the auditorium, listening to the other speakers (because I was fourth), I allowed my weird thoughts to do their thing and present an idea at the last minute. The idea showed up in the form of three simple words: Courage, Happiness, and Gratitude. (No clue why those three words, by the way. I'm sure it had something to do with the events in my life at the time.)

Nonetheless, I took the stage, and started things off by setting a timer on my iPhone for thirty seconds. Then, I hit start. I didn't say a single word on stage for those thirty agonizing seconds (not sure if it was worse for me and my sweaty palms, or the audience and their collective sweaty palms).

When the timer went off, I began to explain what those thirty seconds of unexpected silence signified. I had just created a tiny moment of courage for myself. I owned my weird. Most speakers' worst nightmare is having a mental block on stage and not being able to think of anything to say, with five seconds of silence feeling deadly, never mind a whole half-minute. Yet that's what I had just done . . . and on purpose! It was a demonstration of intentional courage (and temporary discomfort) that I wanted the audience to remember long after my talk.

After the audience shared a collective chuckle (and a sigh of relief), I went on to discuss happiness, sharing the weird morning ritual I'd recently created for myself. Rather than looking at my phone first thing in the morning, I instead had been choosing to handcraft a cup of coffee and read Calvin and Hobbes comics. (There are always a handful of Calvin and Hobbes fans in a large group, so this one went over well.) Starting my day with happiness rather than stress or comparison or negativity (all things social media tends to dish out) had made a huge impact on my overall feelings about my life.

Finally, and this is my favorite part, I actually forgot my third topic and had to ask the audience. With a collective yell, the word "gratitude" shot out of nearly five hundred mouths. (Let me just tell you, that was AWESOME. I made a mental note to forget my final point on stage more often.) I coaxed everyone to pull out their phones, mentioning that most speakers would never want that to happen while on stage. Then (after making a Verizon flip phone joke of some sort for an easy laugh) I prompted everyone to craft an email to one friend or loved one telling them how much they appreciated them. I had everyone simultaneously hit send. In that moment, almost five hundred people sent messages of gratitude to friends and family around the world.

Now let me remind you, this talk was based on *nothing* I had previously prepared. Not a Google Doc or a presentation or a practiced speech—just a reliance on my own weird off-the-cuff-ness and my sincere desire to connect with an audience in an authentic way. These three words weren't groundbreaking theories with expert backing and they weren't strategically mapped to a hero's journey with hand-selected stories to support each point. They were simple, relatable lessons I was discovering in my own weird life.

I share the story with you because this completely impromptu, almost comically simple talk is easily my most memorable, and I still get random emails on a regular basis from people who remember it.

(As a side note, I also had a solid run for a while where I'd do a cartwheel on stage at the end of my talks. I don't recall where this incredibly weird exercise originated, but I thought it would be pretty entertaining for people to see a 6'5", 240-pound man do a cartwheel after talking to them about business or marketing. It always got a great response and I'm proud to say I can still knock out a cartwheel with solid form!)

I admit, my unconventional approach to public speaking has resulted in more than a few raised eyebrows, but it illustrates perfectly the first tenet of the Own Your Weird mindset: embracing your weirdness.

TRUSTING YOUR WEIRD STRENGTHS

See, when I first began my foray into public speaking (this happened accidentally once IWearYourShirt gained traction and organizers started offering to pay me to speak at their events), I would labor over my speaking presentation. I'd tweak every slide in PowerPoint (ew, PowerPoint). I would try to remove witty lines or silly metaphors (removing my weird), thinking people wouldn't take me seriously. I even tried timing some jokes in the beginning. This is what normal public speakers do, right?

Well, none of that stuff ever worked for me. In fact, I could feel the awkwardness in the room when I avoided owning my weird and instead stuck to a mental script I'd created. For years I'd done on-air interviews, created YouTube videos, hosted live video shows, and all of those opportunities were only successful because I relied on my in-the-moment weird impulses and quasi-decent improvisation skills.

Embracing your weirdness means learning to trust your strengths. If you know you do something best in one way and that way doesn't jibe with how things are traditionally done, who cares? In a way, you take a bigger risk by trying to be something you're not because ultimately it's going to come off as insincere. You have to lean in to what your natural talents are, even if they aren't necessarily compatible with the system you're working within. You may come off as "odd" or raise a few eyebrows like I did, but by shifting the rules of whatever game you're playing to fit your weird strengths, you're putting yourself in the best position to succeed.

WEIRD IS MEMORABLE

As I told you, my "three words" speech is one that I still get emailed about to this day. Why? Because it was *weird*; it was unexpected. There were several other times when I was asked to come speak at conferences about marketing or social media, but I found those topics to be far too normal. Sure, I had lots of experience with those things, and I guess you could even say "success." But, I felt that anyone could talk about those topics, and everyone *would* be talking about those topics. I could put my unique spin on them, but the idea of tailoring a talk around those topics bored me to tears, and I knew it would likely bore an audience to tears.

Instead, when a conference organizer would ask for my topic or the name of my talk, I loved replying with something weird like, "T-Shirts, Last Names, and Unicorns" or "The One Talk at This Conference You SHOULD NOT Attend" or "This Isn't a Social Media Talk, It's About Unicorns." (Listen, I had a thing for unicorns, okay? . . . Ah, who am I kidding, I *still* have a thing for unicorns.)

Can you guess what happened with these weird talk titles? The rooms were usually packed. It was often standing-room only. This wasn't because I was some famous person people had heard of. (Heck, I'd ask in my talk if anyone had heard my name before showing up and only a few people would raise their hand. Very humbling for the ol' ego!) People showed up because, as they scanned an event lineup full of "Marketing Tactics This" and "The Future of That" titles all running together, the title of my talk (or my short bio) *stood out*. I was deviating from the norm of what the conference experience typically looked like. I was embracing my desire to avoid giving a talk on a standard topic with a standard name, and I was rewarded with the conference-goers' attention.

This is the power of weirdness. Weird is exciting. Weird is interesting. Weird is memorable. Don't underestimate it.

SHORT-TERM WEIRD
VS. LONG-TERM WEIRD

I will admit, though, we live in a society that gives us two very conflicting messages about whether it's good or bad to be weird.

First, as children, we are encouraged to fit in. When you're in school, even the slightest deviation from the norm can curse you with years of feeling alienated or rejected. Straying from what the other kids do or say or wear or think is risky behavior. (Trust me, as a kid who went to four different high schools and had to make new friends every time, I know this from personal experience.) So we learn to fall in line so we can feel that sense of belonging.

Then, as we get older, society starts lifting up the weird outliers and putting them up on a pedestal. Every famous or successful person you can think of has probably been praised for how unique or interesting or outside-the-norm they are. In fact, their weirdness is actually what helps them cut through the masses; it's what propels them to success. What once was weird is renamed as trailblazing or innovative or amazing.

So, which one is it? Is being seen as "weird" a negative thing or a positive thing?

Well, what I take from this contradiction is that being different can be seen from both a short-term perspective and a long-term perspective. If you can be brave enough to go out on a limb and risk rejection in the short-term, you are actually giving yourself the greatest chance at long-term success.

As accomplished author Seth Godin says, "The long way is the shortcut." If you picked up this book to find the secret to overnight success, you have a better chance of using these random numbers to win the lottery: 4, 8, 15, 16, 23, and 42. (Okay, but if by chance those random numbers do win the lotto, I reserve the right to split the earnings with you.) Being weird is definitely not a key to overnight success. Being weird will require you to take the long route, but that IS the key to getting what you want.

WHAT MAKES YOU WEIRD?

When I thought about writing this book on the theme of owning your weird, the first hesitation I envisioned was someone saying: *But I'm not like you. I don't feel weird or unique.*

This is where I'm gonna have to call bullshit. You know how people make jokes about everyone being a unique snowflake? "Oh, that's cute, you think you're unique," they'll say. With every fiber of my being, I believe we all are unique. We all have the ability to stand out in the world. We all have the ability to own our weird . . . and to prosper because of it.

In fact, being weird is kind of a key component of being human. We're so complex that there's room for every one of us to experience humanness in a different way. Everything about you sets you apart from other people. The way you walk, talk, live, breathe, that really annoying thing you do when you eat (totally kidding . . . or am I?) . . . all of it contributes to your unique signature.

But merely accepting that you're an original isn't enough; you have to actually identify which parts of your originality can be used to your advantage. You have to find your own weirdness, and then embrace it.

One way of doing this is to ask your friends and family. Sure, you're going to get the random sarcastic replies from the less-helpful folks, but you'd be surprised to find out the weird quirks people associate with you. You can grab your phone right now (I'm sure it's very close by) and message five people that you're closest to and ask them what makes you unique. If two people mention the same weird quirk or personality trait or strength, that's definitely something that helps you stand out.

Here are some other questions that might be helpful for figuring out what makes you weird:

- Is there one thing other people constantly ask you for help on?

- What are three words that other people might use to describe you?

- What's one thing you are great at that most people struggle with?

- Do you tend to approach problems in a way that's different from people around you?

Accepting who you are and what makes you *you* may take awhile. Hell, it took me about thirty-three years to get to a place where I felt 100 percent comfortable embracing my weirdness.

Now I wear it like a badge of honor. I know it won't take you thirty-three years, because if you're reading this book you're already searching for it. I simply stumbled into it. Just know that everything you need to succeed on your own terms rests in discovering, accepting, and embracing what sets you apart.

Chapter 1: "Own it!" recap and to-do item

- If you already have an idea of three weird traits that make you *you*, grab a notebook or a journal and write them down. Put a heading at the top of the page that says "Own My Weird!" and list out the three weird traits. If you do NOT have any clue what your weird traits are, use my suggestion to text message five of your friends and ask them what makes you unique/weird. Then, write their answers down in your notebook or journal. Embrace these things. Let them be the things that help you stand out from everyone else in everything you do.

CHAPTER 2

Throw Away the Blueprint

It was 2013, and IWearYourShirt had just shut down. I remember entering a very strange period where I had the unfamiliar feeling of being lost. This crazy T-shirt business had come to define me for so many years, and there I was left with a big question mark about what I was going to do with my life next (not to mention, how I was going to make money).

At about the same time, I was seeing fellow entrepreneurs that I'd known for years popping up in my Facebook news feed promoting these webinars where they were talking about how to turn your skills and knowledge into online courses. Despite my internal compulsion to come up with another big, weird idea to one-up IWearYourShirt, I'll admit that at the time I was just *tired*. Tired of working on something that was hard for people to understand. Tired of trying to figure out how to "scale" (because that's what you're supposed to do in business, right?). Tired of working with clients and answering to other people, which is what IWearYourShirt ended up becoming. I wondered if things would just be easier if I suppressed the impulse to own my weird and instead I followed a clear blueprint that was bringing someone else success in their business.

So, I decided to attend a webinar about how to create and sell an online course. In that webinar I was shown a very specific path, including results from the person hosting the webinar. It was the first time I'd ever heard the phrase "six-figure launch," and of course I was foaming at the mouth. Who doesn't dream of making

$100,000 just by launching something and following the plan laid out by someone who says they've done it? After spending years working long days and clawing for profit a few hundred dollars at a time from over sixteen hundred clients, I was honestly looking for something that would feel easier—and this seemed to be my ticket.

When I finished that webinar, I had spent my $199 on a product guaranteed to give me "everything I needed" to replicate the host's big launch results. I (naively) felt on top of the world. I mean, I had the path to success right in my hands! (Well, really it was just a PDF and some worksheets, so it was more in my *virtual* hands.) Nevertheless, I hunkered down and decided I would create my first online course. *$100,000, here I come!*

I went through all the loops and hoops laid out for me to create my first online course. I pushed aside almost every thought in my mind that I should be doing this in my own weird way and instead tried to follow the plan. I mean, sure, my previous weird ideas had been memorable and generated income, but maybe this step-by-step method was the path to something sustainable and a lot easier? Maybe my *forge-your-own-path* instincts were actually just making business more complicated than it has to be? I literally copied things word-for-word from the PDFs and worksheets (something the creator encouraged us to do) to ensure I would have the same level of success. I pushed aside any inkling to own my weird and put my own spin on this plan.

Then came the launch of my first online course: How to Get Sponsorships for Anything. This was my moment. I followed the blueprint to a T, and I was about to reap the rewards.

Now I'm sure you're wondering . . . how did it all pan out? Where did the plan lead me? Was it the $100,000 I was promised? $200,000?? $13,000,000? (I think you know where this is heading.)

My first course launch brought in just over $5,000.

Now, let me be clear about this: I'm not poo-pooing $5,000. Don't get me wrong, making money from something I created from my own knowledge and experience is a cool feeling. And $5,000 is nothing to scoff at, especially for anyone who's in a tight financial situation. But in the context of following a clearly lit path to a "six-figure launch," it felt like I had failed miserably.

For a split second I went back over my work, comparing it to all my PDFs and step-by-step checklists. Where did I drop the ball? It only took me a second of that line of questioning before I realized the real reason for my wildly different results (a pretty obvious one at that): **I'm a completely different person with a completely different business.**

It sounds stupidly simple, but really think about that statement for a second. People will try to sell you the "proven path" and the "foolproof blueprints" because they CAN. Everyone is looking for a shortcut, and the market is always ripe for people to take advantage of that. I wasn't exhausted after IWearYourShirt closed down because by going my own way I was making things harder on myself; I was exhausted because building a business—especially one that is unique to who you are—is hard freaking work. It's *supposed* to be hard freaking work.

DIFFERENT PARTS, DIFFERENT BLUEPRINT

The reason these business blueprints rarely work is because we're all trying to follow someone else's IKEA instructions when the parts we're holding are for a completely different piece of furniture. You're following the booklet for the Fyrkantig, but you've got all the parts for the Grönkulla (those are real IKEA pieces, by the way).

Humans are complex and nuanced, and so are businesses. Why would we assume there's an easy one-size-fits-all answer to reaching a certain outcome?

Your blueprint is not something you *find*; it's something you *create*. Understanding the truth of this statement is the most basic foundation of the Own Your Weird mindset.

You have to take a look at your own weird parts and pieces—your values, your strengths, your likes and dislikes, the things that make you truly unique, your ideal lifestyle—and figure out what it is you're trying to build. Then—and this is the part people usually don't want to hear—you have to make it up as you go. It's not the silver bullet we're all hoping for, but it's the only method that truly leads you to a life and business that's completely custom to what you have and what you want.

Now, you might think my botched launch was the moment when I hung up my online course coat, that moment when I realized I wasn't going to get the results I had bought into, but you'd be wrong. I'm way too stubborn for that. I continued on, for eight months, launching and promoting and trying to sell my online course, desperately trying to achieve that elusive six-figure number. At the end of the eight months of effort, where did I end up? $32,680 in revenue. That was just revenue, not profit. And while I am not discounting $32,680 as a nominal amount, there was another side effect to my entire first experience in building an online course and following the path laid out by someone else: I was dreadfully unhappy.

Falling short of a goal by doing something risky or creative or unique sucks, but you know what sucks WAY worse? Falling short of a goal because you put your trust in someone else's system or ideas and ignored doing things your own weird way.

I did manage to blow up my online course blueprint and reroute my marketing strategy into something that was way more unique, leveraging this first online course into eventually making over $100,000 with it, but it was NOT because I followed someone else's plan. It was because I turned my head sideways and allowed myself to think: *How can I do this differently? How can I make money from an online course in different ways? How can I sell/promote something and actually not hate that process entirely? What's unique about me and where can I inject my weirdness into every part of this process?*

The result of that reconfiguration was my BuyMyFuture idea where I sold my various courses, software products, AND anything I ever would create in the future for one price. I achieved my "six-figure launch" after all, but it was only because I stopped paying attention to someone else's blueprint and created my own. It was because I owned my weird.

THROWING OUT THE BLUEPRINT IS SOME OF THE BEST MARKETING YOU CAN DO

What I gained from this temporary detour from Own-Your-Weird-Land was a renewed sense of just how crucial it is in marketing to do the opposite of what you see everyone else doing.

Forget for a moment any preconceived notions you have about the word "marketing." Whether you're reading this book because you're a business owner or not, we're all marketers in one way or another. We all have things to promote in our lives—even if it's just the way we present ourselves to the outside world on a daily basis. No idea, business, project, or side hustle can be successful without marketing, which pretty much just boils down to aligning your product with the right customers and making sure they have a reason to buy your product. But just because you need marketing doesn't mean you have to do marketing like everyone else does it. (Eh hem . . . it bears repeating here: the way things have always been done is not the way things have to be done.)

Is it valuable to run a successful Facebook Ads campaign? Yep. Should you buy banner ads or sponsorships if you can get a predictable ROI for your business? Sure. But we all know word-of-mouth is the king of the marketing castle.

Word-of-mouth marketing endures. It endures through time because it is based on the idea of *doing something worth talking about*—something memorable. It's unlikely that five years from now someone will be recalling your Facebook Ads strategy over dinner with friends, but it's entirely possible that someone could still be talking about that off-the-wall weird idea you had that was unlike anything they'd ever seen. Owning your weird isn't just a quick hack; it's a strategy that leaves a lasting impression.

Investing in word-of-mouth marketing by owning your weird is also a good idea because it's the one strategy that can endure the tides of change. Technology continues to morph marketing channels and tactics at a staggering pace. But you know what approach continues to work, regardless of what new mediums and channels emerge? Doing something worth talking about. The power of someone's voice and their desire to share your business with their friends will always win.

I'm fortunate to have listened to the weird voices in my head in 2008. (Not all of them, otherwise this book might have ended up as a romance novel about flying telepathic trolls who inhabit one of Jupiter's moons. I think I'm still gonna keep that idea in my back pocket, though. It's got legs.) I'm proud of how I took on the challenge of creating a completely unique business (and business model) with absolutely no experience with IWearYourShirt. By owning my weird and putting my idea out into the world in 2008, I continue to reap the benefits to this day. You may be reading this book because you'd heard of "the T-shirt guy" on a news segment while getting your oil changed in your car. You may have a friend who told you about "this crazy guy on the Internet who does things you should read about." No amount of money can purchase those types of endorsements. No amount of creative thinking can engineer that outcome on a predictable basis. But, by making the commitment to view everything through the Own Your Weird lens, you can substantially increase the likelihood that word-of-mouth marketing will propel your ideas from a twinkle of a thought to a decade of success.

My entire business, including all of my outside-the-box ideas, would be nothing without the mouths of other people. (Yes, I know that sounds dirty, but stick with me here.) I wasn't a celebrity. I didn't start out with a large following on social media. I started out just like you. With the circle of friends and family that surrounded me. By putting myself and my weird ideas out into the world, I allowed other people with their own circles of friends and family to share my ideas.

The funny part is, we think that fitting in or following the rules will guarantee our success, but all it guarantees is that we become forgettable. Weird ideas may be riskier because they're "unproven" but the payoff is so much greater because you get to be the first of your kind and you get to do it on terms that line up with what you want for your business and life.

YOU ARE NOT A CARBON
COPY OF ANYONE

Now that I've lured you in with the promise of more effective marketing, let's talk about the real reason that ignoring the blueprint is important: **your life is not supposed to be a replica; it's an original.**

There's literally not another person on earth with the same DNA as you. And even if there were, they wouldn't have the same DNA *and* the same experiences. There isn't a person who's lived before you exactly like you, and there won't be anyone after you. That means that the more you try to live your life according to someone else's plan, the more it will be like trying to fit a square peg into a round hole.

What you *can* do is take a little from one person's story and another pinch from someone else and mix it all up into your own completely weird new recipe. You can run every step and every decision through the filter of your unique lens and make sure you're consciously crafting a life that is as original as you are.

This advice even applies to the book you're holding. I hope you didn't pick this up hoping to find a step-by-step plan that you can apply to fix everything in your life and business (spoiler alert: no one can give this to you). What you will find are *my* answers for *my* life, and a framework you can use to find your own. But the most important thing for you to wrap your mind around right out of the gate is that **starting from scratch is the only real way to ensure whatever you end up with is custom-tailored for your DNA.**

Chapter 2: "Own it!" recap and to-do item

- Grab a piece of paper and write down these four words: There is no blueprint. Then, crumple up the paper and throw it away. This is your way of committing to the fact that you are no longer seeking a perfectly laid out plan that doesn't exist. You are ready to create your own weird blueprint (and the coming chapters will help!). If you're an overachiever like me, grab another piece of paper and write "I'm going to own my weird!" and put it somewhere you can see it every day. Let owning your weird become a mantra you embrace on a daily basis.

CHAPTER 3

Know Your Values

By this point we've established that you need to chart your own course rather than blindly follow someone else's. But, if you're going to navigate uncharted waters, it helps to have a compass to guide you through the unexpected twists and turns that are sure to come your way. This is where your values come in.

Remember when I talked about trying to follow someone else's path to make $100K (and failing)? That was one of the first moments in my life where I recognized the feeling of doing something that was not matching up with my values. Of course, I had no idea that's what the feeling was in the moment; I just knew that something was off and it bothered me.

In my experience, that feeling that things are "off" is your gut telling you you're doing something that doesn't match up with your values. But let's back up for a second. What do I even mean when I say values?

Typically when we use the word "values," we do it in reference to the things we care about—the things we consider priorities. We value things like family, our partner, our health, our happiness, etc. However, these kinds of values tend to be very similar across most people. Those are still important things to identify, but they won't necessarily help you answer the more nuanced questions of your life, questions like: What career path is right for me? How do I want to spend my time? What ways do I work best?

The values that will help you answer these questions are what I refer to as your personal values—things you care about that are unique and specific to who you are and what makes you tick. **Your personal values are things you need in order to feel like the best, happiest version of yourself.** Where one person might need laughter and playfulness to feel like themselves, another person might need adventure and exhilaration, and another person might need safety and comfort. Those are the key personal values of those individuals, and they will likely find themselves most happy when they're making decisions that support those needs and priorities.

Now, how do you get clear on what those top values are for YOU? Identifying these things comes naturally to some people, but not to others. For instance, my wife, Caroline, is naturally self-aware and figured out her personal values pretty early on in life. I, on the other hand, took a slightly longer route to get there.

MTV CRIBS GOALS

From a young age we are conditioned to want what society (or family and friends) tell us we *should* want. Whether it's the careers we perceive to be successful (doctors, lawyers, et al.), to the status symbols that we're told will make us feel accomplished (money, material things, awards, etc.), we are conditioned to strive for all of these things, and rarely do we question *why* we're supposed to want them.

For me, as a twenty-something, the things I thought would bring me happiness in life were actually VERY specific. My three big goals were: $1 million in my bank account, a big fancy home (à la *MTV Cribs*, obviously), and a Ferrari I could cruise up and down the streets in. Basically the *Lifestyles of the Rich and Famous* cliché. Many years went by, maybe even a decade, and all I thought I needed to feel successful and fulfilled in life were those three things. (Years later with a little perspective, I'm actually embarrassed writing that last sentence. But, at the time it seemed that clear to me. Money and fancy things = success = happiness.)

Never in my late teens and twenties did I ever ask myself *why* I wanted those things. I just accepted them as the things that I should put all my energy into achieving.

Let's set aside for a moment the fact that those things are superficial and really just ways to prove something to the rest of the world, and let's just evaluate those goals on a practical level. The underlying story of having $1 million and a big house is that it takes a lot of sacrifice to get those things. No one talks about how unbelievably stressful it can be to work fourteen-to-sixteen-hour days or the emotional toll it takes sacrificing your values in order to make a boatload of money.

If you're lucky and you end up getting a bunch of money or a big house, no one else talks to you about the upkeep of both. Usually when you create a system to generate a lot of revenue, there are expenses involved. The more money you make, the more you need to spend to make it (for most of us). I've never owned a million-dollar home of my own, but I owned a "modest" $300,000 one that required continued injections of cash (with zero eventual return).

I imagine you understand the allure of owning a Ferrari, but did you know getting the brakes changed can cost around $10,000 on the *cheapest* of Ferraris? Let's not even think about parking that Ferrari near a single other "normal" car. Cool in theory, but kind of a pain in the butt in reality.

The point is, if you actually take a look at the things we think we're "supposed" to want in life, you start to realize they come with a lot of extra baggage you never considered. You could find yourself so busy striving toward one of these arbitrary goals, making tons of sacrifices along the way, only to one day realize all that sacrifice wasn't even for something that would bring you long-term happiness or satisfaction.

Without identifying your personal values, it's all too easy to focus on possessions or money or status. Those are the things advertisers and social dynamics condition us to want. But once you start to dig in and question every single thing you *think* you want in life, you start to identify the things that bring you happiness from the inside out, regardless of what other people think. That's when you can begin the process of creating your own weird blueprint for a happy and (internally) successful life.

I can guarantee that 100 percent of people reading this book do not need $1 million in their bank account to maintain a happy lifestyle. (And if you do, well how the heck did you end up reading this book!? And also . . . your spending habits are beyond out of control.) Of course we all need money. Yes, you need a roof over your head. And yeah, you probably need some form of transportation. But what are all the other things in life that bring you joy on a day-to-day basis? Things like time with your family, time for exercise, time for hobbies, flexibility in your daily schedule, the ability to choose work that you actually enjoy. Those are just a few examples, but they are the examples of the things that are the foundation in the drawing of the blueprint of my life.

The most important thing is not just in identifying what you want, but why you want it. If the answer is that you want it to look cool or accomplished to other people, it's probably not the best indication of your true values. But if you want something because it makes you feel like yourself *despite* what anyone else thinks, that just might be the answer to what you care about deep down.

Like I said, these things aren't always obvious to everyone, so here are some questions that might help lead you to what those personal values are.

Questions for uncovering your values:

- What are things you love doing? What are things you hate doing? Now ask yourself why you love or hate those things? Are there any patterns or similarities that might point to what you value?

- When do you feel most *at ease*? In contrast, what situations make you feel the most tense or *anxious*? Again, look for patterns here. If it makes you anxious, chances are it's because of a lack of one of your personal values.

- What activities feel most natural to you?

- What does your ideal day look like?

Remember, your personal values are **things you need in order to feel like the best, happiest version of yourself.** You may say you're happy as long as you know where your health insurance is coming from, so you'd choose a value like "stability." Or that it's important to live near your family and spend quality time with them, then you'd choose "family/community." Or you absolutely need one hour per day to daydream in your art studio and paint freely with zero judgment or expectations, in which the core value of "creativity" matters a ton to you. Other values could be things like: adventure, nature, service, flexibility, security, community, growth, structure, impact, humor, leadership, or optimism. The list goes on and on. Once you start to identify what these things are, that's when you can reevaluate your goals to see if they are based on what you think the world expects of you, or what deep down you want and need to be happy.

MY TOP 3 VALUES

So how did *I* discover what my values were? Well, for starters, I paid attention. I used my life and business experience to notice when things felt "off" and to identify situations or scenarios where I felt like my happiest, most Jason-y self. After years of trial and error, I discovered three things that are central to what I need in my life and my business(es).

VALUE #1: CONTROL

The word "control" sometimes gets a bad rap. This value for me is not as much about needing to control everything or everyone as it is about self-determination. I know now that I need the ability to influence the outcomes in my own life and business in order to feel happy. Some people feel the opposite. Some people struggle with having all the pressure on them or taking the reins, so they'd rather be in a more supportive role in situations where they may not have complete control of their destiny, but they also don't have the weight of it all on their shoulders, either.

This value became incredibly clear to me through my experience trying to scale IWearYourShirt. By 2011, I had grown my IWearYourShirt business from one T-shirt wearer (me) to a company of eight people. Each day, five shirt wearers (including myself) wore a T-shirt for a company and promoted that company via social media. Each person took photos in the shirt, recorded a YouTube video in the shirt, and hosted a live video show in the shirt.

Before, when it was just me, I could 100 percent control the outcome every day. I knew how hard I'd work, what my standards were for my videos, and how I would interact with our fans. But, unfortunately, by the time we scaled to more shirt wearers, those things became beyond my control. Looking back, I definitely could have communicated expectations and been a better manager, but still, relinquishing the control of the daily operations of the business proved to be way more stressful for me than I ever anticipated.

Some business owners want the growth more than they want to control the outcome. They're willing to loosen those reins a bit and just trust because they know they value what's to gain even more (money, notoriety, impact, etc.). But what I've learned about myself is that's *not* a trade I'm willing to make. I would rather give up those things (more revenue and more employees) in order to keep my complete autonomy. Trying to grow a company like a fancy Silicon Valley startup would make me feel physically ill (unless, maybe, that startup was Pied Piper?). I didn't know that until I experienced the negative feelings that came along with going against my values.

One of the most important tools to finding what works for you and what feels right is in identifying the things you *don't* enjoy doing. Paying attention to those feelings (both negative and positive) clued me in to this value of control that I now use as a compass to navigate my decisions moving forward. It's why I keep all my businesses intentionally small, agile, and with as much ownership and autonomy as I can.

VALUE #2: FLEXIBILITY

My second "core value" (as Caroline has taught me to call them) is flexibility, but it has nothing to do with yoga poses. Yes, your health is important, and yoga is great for your body, but let's stay focused on business here. (Fine, okay, let's all pause for a quick downward-facing dog. Did you do it? Bonus points to anyone who does a downward dog and sends me a photo of you doing yoga with my book.)

What I *actually* mean when I say flexibility in relation to business is making decisions that leave you some wiggle room. I need the ability to easily and quickly shift in the moment, based on whatever the changing circumstances might be. I find that control and flexibility tend to be very closely related for me. I want the ability to affect the outcomes in my own business and life (control) AND I want the ability to affect those outcomes whenever I want based on changing circumstances (flexibility.)

Using flexibility as a value on my compass is sometimes as simple as keeping a flexible work schedule (and going to the movies on a Monday morning), or it sometimes shows up in a bigger way, like in our decision to rent instead of buy a house when we moved from Florida to California.

We moved across the country years ago now and we've considered buying something and putting down roots. However, right now at this stage of our lives, that ability to move or travel whenever the mood strikes us is incredibly vital to our happiness. Most often, this value of flexibility shows me what decision NOT to make. Whether it's in comes from this one source.

You may have seen this one coming from the T-shirt-wearing, last-name-selling guy, but truthfully, as of writing this book, if I'm confronted with a decision that's going to lock me in to something long-term or create a structure that can't evolve, it's probably not the right move. (The one exception to this would be marriage. See, Caroline, I love you so much that marrying you outweighs my flexibility value!).

VALUE #3: ORIGINALITY (A.K.A. OWNING MY WEIRD)

Surprise, surprise. The entire premise of the book you're reading is based on the thing that I consider to be most central to my personality. This core value has only been at the forefront of my decision-making processes for the past year or so. Sure, it's been hiding under the surface for basically my whole life, but only recently have I recognized how crucial it is in steering me toward decisions that are actually fulfilling.

Those few years after SponsorMyBook but before BuyOurFuture when I was making online courses, I couldn't figure out why I was making good money but still struggling to feel fulfilled. I was making things and building an audience, with 100 percent control of the outcome and complete flexibility, yet something still felt missing. This was especially obvious when I tried following someone else's blueprint to financial success. It wasn't just because I didn't get the results I was promised; it was because I was disappearing into the herd. I never want to fall back into that "state of beige" like I did all those years ago, which is when I realized that whatever I endeavor to do—both in life and in business—it HAS to feel original. It has to feel at least a little bit weird and uniquely, authentically me.

PERSONAL VALUES VS. BUSINESS VALUES

You might notice that I mentioned these three values in the context of both my business and my life. You might also be asking yourself, is there a difference between identifying your personal values vs. your business values? The ultimate goal is to have these two things completely overlap, especially if you're a small business owner or a solopreneur. Your business and brand will feel the most authentic if your business values are in complete alignment with what you value personally—and you'll likely find that running your business is the most fulfilling that way. When your business allows you to work in a way that makes you feel most YOU, that's when it feels less like a job and more like an extension of a life that you already love.

YOUR VALUES SHOULD
MAKE YOU FEEL THINGS

One thing that also helps me use these values as my compass is to associate each of my values with a feeling.

My value of control makes me feel empowered. No longer do I feel like my businesses and my ideas have a life of their own, like they have the power to stress me out or run my life. Sure, I don't control everything, and plenty of stuff goes wrong. But I do have enough control that I can sleep at night without the stress of what the next day will bring.

My value of control also makes me feel like I'm always able to evolve. No matter what's going on, no matter how many customers I have (or don't have) for a project, and no matter what anyone else is doing in my "industry," I can make a change and do things my way.

My value of flexibility makes me feel free. It allows me to not only start multiple different projects and scratch my various creative itches but it also allows me to have the freedom to bounce around every day of my life whenever the mood strikes me. While that might drive you nuts, I thoroughly enjoy being able to dip from one project to the next at a moment's notice.

My value of owning my weird makes me feel alive. It makes me feel the warm and fuzzies when I come up with a new weird idea. It fuels me to push myself further with every project I take on. And the self-guiding question: "am I owning my weird and doing this differently?" always hits me first when I start anything new. It's the one value that makes me feel the most . . . ME.

You probably have different values than I do. You may crave community, honesty, creativity, stability, and lots of other things. That's great! I want you to discover your own core values. I want you to find the things that light you up. I want you to have these values top of mind for you at all times. And just like the eco-friendly paper filters I use on my Chemex coffee maker every morning, I want you to filter every single decision you make through these values.

The eighteen-year-old version of me didn't care about values. There's probably no way I could have convinced that former JNCO-jeans-wearing version of myself to establish a list of things that would become filters for decision-making. However, I now believe I could have avoided a lot of mistakes and tons of detours that led me to dead ends in my early entrepreneurial life had I created a set of values to use as decision-making filters. When it's said and done, I'm glad I made the mistakes I made; they brought me to this moment. But hindsight is and always will be 20/20, and if I can spare you some of the time and effort that I spent getting offtrack, then that's what I'm here for.

Here's a beautiful thing about life that I want you to think about throughout this book: you can change your life to fit your values right now. You can uproot your current thought processes and beliefs. You can figure out what really matters to you and start changing everything, one tiny decision at a time. Imagine how different your life might feel if everything around you—the people, the possessions, the routines, the activities—were selected based on what truly makes you feel the most happy. That kind of life 100 percent exists. (I know because I get to live it.)

Just like finding success in business, finding your core values isn't going to happen with a path created by someone else. You have to stop looking outward at what everyone is telling you to want and instead look inward for what feels true (and weird) to you. Once you do, you have the most powerful navigating tool there is, and trust me, the right decisions will start to become a lot easier to make.

Chapter 3: "Own it!" recap and to-do item

• Can you guess this one, you savvy reader, you? Yep, we're going to do ninety minutes of hot yoga together! Oh wait, that's not it. You're going to do your best to come up with your three core values. These may not be perfect out of the gates, but the values that jump out at you immediately are the ones that probably dictate your life decisions the most right now. Write these down. Then, if you are feeling a bit weird, take a photo doing a downward dog yoga pose next to your core values and email it to me (or better yet, post it on social media and tag me @jasondoesstuff in the photo!).

CHAPTER 4

Get Comfortable
with Rejection

Here's a key piece of owning your weird I want to make sure I don't gloss over: people aren't always going to "get it." Writing your own blueprint based on your values usually means taking a risk by straying from the norm, and people's brains tend to short-circuit a bit when they encounter something that goes beyond what they've seen before.

When I started IWearYourShirt, that was my first big leap into the deep end of owning my weird, and I experienced my fair share of people who didn't get it. It first showed up when people told me not to "quit my day job." (Oops, too late.) Those people weren't jerks trying to crush my dreams; they were actually well-intentioned people looking out for me and trying to keep me safe.

But, those early criticisms of IWearYourShirt from my friends and family were actually pretty mild compared to the backlash I started to get in the form of online comments about IWearYourShirt. One particular example that I'll never forget was when someone shared IWearYourShirt on Digg.com. (Digg.com used to be a popular place to find and discuss anything going on in the world, often times with a technology slant similar to what is now Reddit.)

By the time I noticed the humongous spike in web traffic, the post on Digg had amassed a ton of comments. As you might imagine, what with the Internet being like criticism on steroids, not all of those comments were loving messages of encouragement. In fact, when I finally discovered the post, there were fifty-five comments on the thread, and fifty-three of them were negative. The other two were unrelated spam.

I'd like to say I didn't care, but honestly I was hurt. (Well, actually I was pissed. But, looking back with more self-awareness, I can see that pissed and defensive actually equaled hurt.) Here I was trying to put this weirdly unique idea out into the world, trying to share something different and unusual, and I was being ridiculed for it. For the first ten to fifteen minutes after reading through the comments, I sulked. I sat on my couch, staring at the website on my laptop, seriously wondering if I should just quit. Was I stupid for trying this T-shirt thing? And even if I wasn't, was it worth all the negativity I was getting for even trying? Should I stop embracing my weirdness so I can avoid painful moments like this in the future?

Reading that right now, it sounds ridiculous. How could I possibly allow the opinions of fifty-three strangers (and two spammers) cause me to question myself and my ideas to the point of quitting? I didn't know these people. They didn't even exist in my mind until that exact moment. How could I even come close to letting them inflict so much pain and self-doubt?

After about an hour and a half of fluctuating between fuming and sulking, I felt a rush of emotions come over me. *Who are these people to take control of my life and make me feel like I should stop going down the road I've started paving for myself?*

These people DID NOT matter to me prior to that experience. Why in the world would I let their opinions affect me? Sure, I couldn't just erase the feelings they caused, but I didn't have to give them the power to derail my progress. To crush the confidence and courage I'd mustered up to put myself and my idea out there.

I'd like to be able to say at this point that I slammed my laptop closed and screamed "THIS. IS. SPARTAAAA!" and went on to work even harder on IWearYourShirt without giving another thought to those Internet trolls. But, I didn't. I hadn't learned yet how to ignore comments like that. So I did what all level-headed people do when they've been attacked on the Internet: I engaged the trolls by responding. (Note: as a general rule of thumb, DO NOT engage the trolls.) I felt like I had to stand up for myself, so I responded to just a few handful of comments on that Digg post, especially ones that made personal jabs, explaining that I was a human being and that I wasn't going to allow these random strangers—who had never tried to put themselves out there—to impede my progress. THEN, I shut my laptop!

I'm guessing you've had a version of this story happen to you in your life. You've put yourself out there in some way. You've gone out on some limb. You've tried to let your weirdness and difference shine through, and a bunch of idiots (or maybe just one) tried to snuff it out like a Yankee Candle at the end of a nice book club gathering. Well, congrats, you've joined the super-not-so-elite club of people who've encountered criticism or rejection (a.k.a. everyone who ever lived). I've been there. You've been there. Did we just become best friends? Yep!

Risking rejection is simply the price of entry for pursuing a life that's uniquely suited to what makes you happy.

As I said, if you're writing your own blueprint, you're likely deviating from the norm, and people that don't have the courage to do the same might respond with words or actions that hurt. But, trust me, the price is WELL worth the ultimate reward of building a life or business you love. If you can learn to weather the storm and build resilience to these kinds of comments and criticism, you are the one with the last laugh.

My time as an entrepreneur has not been all sunshine and rainbows, but I'm glad it hasn't. The difficult moments of sharing my differences and putting my uniqueness out into the world have shaped me into the person I am today. Without the small battles, like dealing with fifty-three trolls on Digg, I wouldn't have taken another step toward self-acceptance, another inch toward embracing myself completely. I wouldn't have had the courage to keep putting unique ideas out into the world, which I now know to be crucial to my happiness. I would have stopped owning my weird and you wouldn't be reading this book right now.

We all crave validation. That's natural. But if you're forging your own path and owning your weird it's extremely important that you learn to seek validation and take feedback from the right sources. If you pay attention to every naysayer that you encounter, you'll just be pulled right back into the herd.

If you want to start owning your weird more, you have to expect most feedback to be negative. People will always criticize what they don't understand. Most criticism of you or your ideas will be from people who are judging you based on a very narrow, limited view of reality. All they can see or understand is what is inside the proverbial box. You, on the other hand, are trying to expand reality, trying to expand the proverbial box, so it's hard to make sense of that.

But does that mean you should ignore all feedback completely? How do you know which voices to listen to and which ones to ignore?

FEEDBACK CAN BE DANGEROUS

For the most part, musicians create their songs and albums in isolation. It's not uncommon to have an artist drop off the map for a year or two, then out of nowhere come out with a chart-topping album garnering multiple hits, copious amounts of radio play, and appearances galore. We, as consumers of music, rarely ever see any iteration or minimum viable versions of a musician's songs—only the final product.

This is very different than the business world, and especially the online business world, where it's customary to put up an early version of an idea, take in customer feedback, and use that feedback to go forward and improve your product.

Despite how important it is to share your work and listen to customer feedback, seeing how the music industry works has made me wonder if there are potential benefits to working in isolation the way musicians do. Can letting people into your work and process too early on be detrimental to your end product? From experience I can tell you the answer is yes.

Listen, I understand that music is art and you might think that art is different from business. However, like art, if you're owning your weird with your business, you're likely going to ruffle some feathers. Great musicians are always trying to push their body of work (and music itself) forward with each album they put out, which means there is inevitably some backlash from fans when the first few singles of a new album are released. Some people expect more of the same and when they're met with a style of music or sound that is unfamiliar, they don't know what to do.

The same thing can happen when you're owning your weird in business. People are used to one thing and when they see you pushing things forward or pioneering a new path, it's uncomfortable. Of course the natural reaction will be to criticize. Which is why you have to be careful what feedback you take in. It can be beneficial sometimes to create in relative isolation like a musician if you have faith in your idea but you know it will take a while for others to come around. In fact, when you're forging a new path, sometime feedback is actually dangerous.

How do you know when you're ready for feedback? And who should you seek out for the most beneficial and constructive criticism?

Do you want to get feedback from your ideal customers? Absolutely. Do you want to get feedback from someone who has created something similar to what you're building? Yes, that could definitely be helpful.

Do you want to get feedback from a friend, family member, or acquaintance on social media who has no experience with what you're building and who won't be your potential customer? NO. That is dangerous feedback.

When receiving any feedback, look at it through this very important lens, which we can frame as a couple questions:

- Is this person my potential (or existing) customer?

- Does this person have experience in my industry and should I trust their opinion?

- Is the product or service I'm sharing actually ready for feedback?

Feedback has a tenth-degree black belt in the art of derailing progress. Even when I was a kid, I did my best to make sure someone's feedback never stopped me from embracing my weirdness. Whether it's due to DNA or to being a child of the 80s (thank you, Trapper Keeper!), I'll never know, and it doesn't matter. The point is to make sure feedback doesn't knock you offtrack of owning your weird.

FEEDBACK AS PROCRASTINATION

Feedback can also be a vehicle for avoiding doing the actual work. I know there have been many times in my entrepreneurial career when I had a huge task ahead of me, and because it was daunting, I'd instead share work I'd already done with friends to get positive reinforcement.

For many creators and entrepreneurs, that singular moment could be the roundhouse kick that completely stops a project in its tracks (like Chuck Norris, swinging his beautiful denim-covered leg at your face). They don't get the support they were searching for and instead they get criticized.

Early stages of building and creating can be very vulnerable. You don't have thick enough mental armor to block the attacks of feedback. Especially from non-credible sources. When a musician is working on their music, they take advice from experienced writers, producers, and fellow musicians. They certainly aren't asking someone who's never heard their music or has zero experience in their industry for feedback. Even though musicians care about their fans, they most certainly aren't asking the fans what they want.

Like Henry Ford found in the early 1900s when trying to build the first consumer automobile, "If you had asked people want they wanted, they would have said faster horses." Had Ford listened to his potential customers, he may never have built the Model T and revolutionized transportation forever. (My weird brain immediately imagines horses with jetpacks. That sounds fun!)

We should follow this same advice for our businesses. Take feedback from sources that have experience in what we are trying to do or build. Seek those people out first. Build a trust circle of people around us from whom we should be taking feedback. Finish creating something without the thoughts and comments of ultra-crepidarians (yep, you just learned a new word, you're welcome!).

The next time you get feedback—whether you asked for it or not—ask yourself the questions above. If the feedback doesn't fit, then don't waste a single moment with it. If it does, apply it (using your own good judgment, of course) and keep working on whatever weird new project you're building.

WHEN FEEDBACK IS HELPFUL

When I started working on the online course–creation platform I co-founded (Teachery), it was important to me to validate this idea early on and get feedback from people that might use the software. I didn't want to invest all the time to build the software if no one was ever going to pay for it. So I created a simple email capture page (it didn't even have a logo on it!) with a few sentences that clearly explained what Teachery would be and why it would be valuable, making it clear that this was geared toward online course creators.

I shared that email capture page on my various social media accounts, to an existing email list I had, and with a handful of friends who I knew were thinking about creating (or had created) online courses. Within a few weeks of promotion, I had around a hundred email addresses of people I could start getting feedback (and potentially criticism) from.

The first few emails that were sent to those hundred people completely shaped the first version of Teachery. Sure, I had my own creative ideas, but I also had a hundred people whom I wanted to hear from and who might have problems that I could try to solve. The important thing to note about these hundred people is that they opted in for a specific thing I was working on. They raised their hands and said "please tell me more about online courses!" They weren't just a random group of people who may never build an online course (or worse, people who didn't even know what an online course was).

The feedback and criticism from the folks on this email list were very helpful. It not only showed myself and my co-founder, Gerlando Piro, what features were the most necessary to launch Teachery with, but it also helped us decide what features we never wanted to build (due to complexity, or just our own beliefs about creating an online course). The goal wasn't to accept and use feedback from every person; the goal was to have a pool of criticism and suggestions that we could pull from.

I continue to use a prelaunch page for almost every single project I work on. I like to create a very focused email list of people who want more information about whatever I'm working on (which I've clearly explained on the prelaunch page). This helps ensure that every project I launch will have a list of interested people who opted in to hear more about that specific idea. If you do a good job of explaining what your idea is, it can be a fantastic way to get feedback from the right source. But, it's only useful if you learn how to take any criticism with a grain of salt, consider the source, and ultimately get comfortable with the fact that not everyone will understand what you're doing.

RUNNING TOWARD REJECTION

Encountering people who don't understand what you're doing is the short-term price for standing out. That's why it's essential to develop ways to deal with rejection and not let it stop you. Not only have I figured out how to handle rejection (I've had lots of practice), but in a weird way I have actually come to find it useful; it helps me gauge whether or not I'm doing something truly unique. I now run toward it rather than away from it because it's a clear sign I'm stepping outside of what's expected. I'm owning my weird!

If you're someone who takes rejection especially hard, try reframing it in this positive way. Start trying to see criticism as a win. For every negative comment or family member who doesn't quite get it, just imagine that you're getting all kinds of Own Your Weird points that you are going to be able to cash in for fun prizes like happiness, contentment, personal satisfaction, and an oversized stuffed teddy bear (wearing a sweet Hawaiian shirt, obviously).

WHO'S THE BOSS?

I share the tips above because I know that no matter how many times I say "don't pay attention to what people think about you," we are all human and just want to be accepted. It's incredibly difficult to ignore that desire to fit in, and hence the pain that can come with feeling like you don't fit in. But, at some point, you do have to decide who the boss is.

Whose opinion is going to matter more—theirs or yours? Or, in other words, is it worth living a life that doesn't make you truly happy just to please other people?

You have to reach a point where the long-term satisfaction and happiness of living an authentic life outweighs the short-term discomfort or pain of feeling silly, rejected, misunderstood, or criticized. It's time to stop living for other people—your parents, your boss, Digg trolls, whoever—and start living for you.

Chapter 4: "Own it!" recap and to-do item

- Have you been sitting on a weird or unique idea for awhile but don't think people will actually care about it (or buy something from you)? My challenge to you is to create a dead-simple landing page for your idea that explains the pain point your idea is going to solve for someone. Then, add a simple email capture on the page where people can sign up to learn more if they're interested. Don't be afraid to own your weird in the copy of this page! Then, share this page on your various social media channels and email it to a few friends and family. Even if you only get a handful of email subscribers, guess what just happened? You reached Validation Stage 1 of your idea! Huzzah! It's gone from a thought in your head to an idea people are raising their hands for and you might want to consider moving forward with! Yay you! (Bonus points: Email me your landing page so I can take a look at it.)

CHAPTER 5

Think Opportunities, Not Obstacles

Aside from potential criticism and the opinions of other people, there are always going to be challenges that come with forging your own path and owning your weird. In my case, after hanging up my final T-shirt in 2013, a dark cloud hovered over any thought or discussion involving IWearYourShirt. Sure, the business had generated more than $1 million during its five-year tenure, but I didn't have any of that money left; in fact, I was over $100,000 in debt. That debt didn't happen overnight, it came from having a business where the beginning of the year brought in lower revenue (remember the pricing structure of $1, $2, $3 per day, etc?) but I still had the same amount of expenses regardless of the amount of revenue (that's what having employees and fixed costs will do to you). In 2011 I started to get behind on payables to vendors we were working with and had to use credit cards to have enough cash to pay employee salaries. Before I knew it $5,000 borrowed here and there quickly added up to that scary number. It sucked. I didn't even like to bring up money in conversations about IWearYourShirt because I felt such shame about the financial situation I (and really, the business) had gotten into.

The truth is, I saw IWearYourShirt as my biggest business failure, and it was painful to think about. When you do something for five years and pour your heart, soul, and nearly every waking hour into it, it's not an easy thing to detach from. It's even harder to detach from the negative thoughts and memories that are left over when it's gone.

Thanks to a random coincidence, around this same time, I picked up a book that would completely change the way I saw this "failure." Now, it's important to note that I'm not a guy who likes to speak in absolutes. You know, when people say things like "this is the worst day ever!" or "this is the best deep-fried Twinkie on planet Earth!" It's not something I tend to do in my own life, and it can cause me cringe worthy feelings when other people do it. That said, I can unequivocally state with absolute certainty that the most important book I've ever read is Ryan Holiday's *The Obstacle Is the Way*.

"THE OBSTACLE IS THE WAY"

The premise of this most-important-book-I've-ever-read revolves around the idea of stoicism. Google tells me the definition of stoicism is "the endurance of pain or hardship without a display of feelings and without complaint."

I want it to be clear that I haven't become an emotionless robot because I read Holiday's book. (On the contrary, I was probably more of an emotionless robot *before* reading his book.) *The Obstacle Is the Way* walks you through stories of stoicism from business owners, the über-successful, and war heroes. But I didn't read this book because I was interested in becoming more like any of the people in the book. I just wanted something that would help me finally overcome the emotional baggage of shutting down my business.

About a third of the way through the book, I started to see the light. I could begin to understand that having this unfortunate ending to the story of IWearYourShirt was not what defined the business, my idea, or five years of my life. It especially didn't define who I was as a person. That ending was simply a stepping stone to something else. Sure, it was a stepping stone that hurt, stressed me out, and left me angry at times. But it wasn't the final stepping stone. It was actually a very important piece of my entrepreneurial journey that taught me a lot.

In *The Obstacle Is the Way*, Ryan Holiday says:

"Never forget, within every obstacle is an opportunity to improve our condition."

Progress isn't made while sitting comfortably on your laurels. Change usually doesn't happen unless something gets in the way that needs to be dealt with. As I've looked back on some of the most pivotal moments in my life, what I've come to realize is that without obstacles, I wouldn't have become a better person or business owner. I actually *needed* each obstacle or challenge to show me I had room to improve or that something was wrong that needed fixing. These things were, as Ryan puts it, opportunities to improve my condition.

Ever since reading Ryan's book, I continue to come back to the phrase "***opportunities, not obstacles***" as a reminder of why challenges are necessary, and yes, even worth celebrating. Every time I encounter a setback, whether it's as big as a failed business idea, or as small as an angry customer email that derails my day, I repeat that mantra. I look for whatever way I can to use that obstacle as a learning experience or an opportunity to take a new turn in my own path.

TURNING MY OBSTACLE INTO AN OPPORTUNITY

Finishing *The Obstacle Is the Way* gave me new perspective at a time when I needed it the most. While the shift didn't happen overnight, I started to feel differently about everything much quicker than I thought. It started with rewriting some of the thoughts in my head. I would repeat these things to myself:

IWearYourShirt was not a complete failure.

You, Jason, are not a complete failure.

You, Jason, are not just IWearYourShirt.

You, Jason, *can* come up with more ideas and *will* go on to do other things.

You, Jason, could always just get a job at Target or Starbucks and figure out a way to get by in life.

> You, Jason, could always move home, suck it up for a bit, and remember that nothing is permanent.

> You, Jason, need to stop talking to yourself in third person. It's freaking people out.

It sounds silly, but Ryan's book gave me the permission I needed to be more accepting of myself and the missteps I had made. More important, it also gave me story after story and example after example of people who had screwed up WAY worse than I had and had bounced back, too.

Now, unfortunately, I have to drop another absolute on you. (Ugh, I'm such a rule breaker of my own rules.) Writing my first book, *Creativity for Sale,* was the most cathartic thing I've ever done because I was able to let go of the mental baggage revolving around failure. The only reason that book got written (and the subsequent catharsis even happened) was because IWearYourShirt failed. Had it kept going, I would have kept going. I would not have gone through the exercise of writing a book and would not have experienced the personal Emotional Gymnastics Championships that ultimately led me to becoming a happier person. The obstacle (shutting down IWearYourShirt) was just a stepping stone to writing a book, a process that opened me up as a person and transformed my life.

I can look at every situation I've been in and every business I've created, even before IWearYourShirt, and clearly see an obstacle that led to the beginning of each business. Some problem. Some issue. *Something* that needed to be overcome.

My mom's divorce left me with a last name I no longer wanted, which sparked the idea for my BuyMyLastName project where I auctioned off my last name to the highest bidder (remind you, netting me nearly $100,000).

When I set out to create my first online course, I searched high and low and couldn't find a course platform that suited my needs. Everything was either too bloated with features, too difficult to set up, or worst of all, forced me to install something technical and fancy on my existing website. I didn't have the time or energy to fight a technical uphill battle, I just wanted my online course to exist for people to enjoy! Stumbling into that obstacle was what led to the creation of a new software company, Teachery, which is an online course platform I co-own with my friend Gerlando Piro.

Opportunities, not obstacles. These roadblocks exist for a number of reasons: to alter our path, teach us something we'll need on the journey ahead, or simply to create a much more interesting and adventurous ride. The sooner you can begin to see your own challenges as opportunities, the happier and more motivated you'll be.

WHAT OBSTACLE CAN YOU TURN INTO AN OPPORTUNITY?

You, most likely, are staring an obstacle in the face right now. How can you change your perspective on whatever that obstacle is?

Did your website go down on launch day? Truly a bummer. I've been there (many times). Can you use it as a teaching moment for anyone who looks up to you for inspiration? Can you use it as a moment to reward your loyal customers and extend some offer to them that wouldn't have existed? Can you learn from the experience if you have the right customers for your business (ones that don't scurry like bugs when the lights get turned on at the sight of any problems with your business)?

Did you end a long-term relationship? Also, truly a bummer and one I've experienced. Could this open the doors for you to find someone who is better suited for the person you've become (or weird person you've always been)? Does this allow your former partner to do the same thing (find someone they are a better match for)? Does it create the opportunity for both of you to live happier and healthier lives?

Did you close down a business that isn't doing well? I don't even think I need to say much else here. Won't ending this business open doors of opportunity elsewhere that have been closed or set aside for too long? (The answer is yes, and I can obviously attest to that.)

Obstacles suck. They are not fun. They are not ice cream cones covered in fudge and sprinkles. They are plates of boiled, unseasoned vegetables. They are the difficult decisions we must make in our lives. They are the important decisions hiding behind awful events and circumstances. When you're in the middle of dealing with an obstacle, it will feel like climbing Mount Everest. And even though you and I will probably never know that exact feeling, we can sure as hell take a wild guess at how difficult it would be.

Like climbing Everest, you overcome obstacles step by step. You put one foot in front of the other. You swing your pickaxe into the next piece of frozen mountain and you move forward.

There will always be more obstacles. But as Holiday talks about in his book, and as stoicism teaches, if you can endure the temporary pain and hardship, and see it for exactly that, you can take a step back and not let it stop you. With every new obstacle that comes your way, you have the experiences of the obstacles you've previously endured and overcome to guide you. They will remind you to take a deep breath. To zoom out. To realize today isn't "the worst day ever."

You don't have to adopt stoicism to see the value in honoring the obstacle. But you do need to realize that once you've begun your journey (and hey! that's a huge step!), the only way out of the pain or challenge is through it. This is the best recipe I've found for turning lemons into lemonade, and coming out the other end of the obstacle wiser and more equipped for the next big adventure.

Owning Your Weird means going off-road. If you're not following someone else's path, that means there are no well-worn tracks to guide you. There is no one that has gone before you to smooth out your way and remove all those inevitable obstacles. YOU are going to have to be the one to do that for yourself. But, if you can start to see that process as an essential part of creating your own happiness, and learn to take in each challenge as an opportunity for something positive, then you can power through and experience the awesome benefits that accompany living life on your own terms.

Chapter 5: "Own it!" recap and to-do item

- What obstacle have you had in your life recently that you need to let go of? That you need to give yourself permission to move on from and to see as an opportunity to improve your life in some way? This one will feel especially empowering when you confront this obstacle, morph it into an opportunity, and shout at the tippy-top of your lungs, "I OWNED IT!"

CHAPTER 6

Test Your Assumptions

You know what they say about assumptions . . . they suck. (What's that? You thought I was gonna make a joke about "making an ass out of U and ME?" Yes, well, that applies, too.) Even if you're not completely sold on this whole Own Your Weird thing yet, if there's one thing I hope you'll take from this book it's how important it is to test your assumptions.

Phrases like "I don't think this will work" or "No one will buy my product" are assumption-based. It's a future outcome our brains have decided is likely. But rarely do we stop to wonder why our brains have predicted that outcome. Is it because we have evidence to back these predictions up? Or is it because we're afraid and we're choosing to protect ourselves from failing by not even trying?

Our brains have this mystical, magical, commanding power over us. It can be incredibly difficult to challenge our own thoughts. Even if we have data from other sources, we often still can't get past our own mental barriers. I'd like to tell you I've come up with a perfect framework to never let your assumptive thoughts dictate your decisions again. But I don't. Maybe someone way smarter than me does, but all I have to share is a list of endless positive things that have come as a result of my own assumption-challenging experiences.

ASSUMPTIONS ABOUT STARTING YOUR NEXT BUSINESS/PROJECT/WHATEVER

I'm amazed at how often I hear from people who are talking themselves out of being successful. (By the way, when I say "successful," please know that this is a term you must define for yourself, and should not be based on any outside metrics. More on that in Section III, but for now, we'll just simply define "success" as accomplishing whatever it is you set out to do).

Within these messages and emails are phrases like:

- "My idea has already been done before."

- "I'm not special, why would anyone care what I have to say?"

- "I don't have the skills required to make my idea happen."

- "I can't make money doing what I want to do."

- "I don't know where to start."

Let's challenge each of these assumptions together before we move forward so we can both agree to see them for what they are, which is either untrue or simply excuses. I'm hoping this will teach you how to break down your own assumptions and challenge that stubborn brain each time it tries to talk you out of doing what you actually want to do.

"MY IDEA HAS ALREADY BEEN DONE BEFORE."

AWESOME! This is an assumption that could easily be true, but it only means the market is proven for your product or service. People are already paying for it. That's actually a good thing. There are virtually ZERO truly new ideas left. Our species is too smart. Everything is just a remix of other ideas at this point. That's okay, too. Embrace what makes your remix of an idea unique.

"I'M NOT SPECIAL, WHY WOULD ANYONE CARE WHAT I HAVE TO SAY?"

Whoever told you that you weren't special was an asshole. You are special. I am special. We are all special little snowflakes, okay? (If you need more convincing, just see **Chapter 1, "Embracing Your Weirdness."**)

Now that we've gotten that out of the way, it's also important to keep in mind that being "special" is only *part* of what's going to help you succeed. No one lines up to buy the newest iPhone or pair of Air Jordans just because Steve Jobs or Phil Knight are special people. Yes, Apple and Nike's success is due *in part* to the special (weird) DNA from Jobs and Knight that's baked into their brands, but it's also their blood, sweat, tears, work, sacrifices, failures, mistakes, and assumption-testing thinking that leads you to buy the product they're producing. It's uniqueness meets talent meets effort, and effort is the part of that equation that is most within your control. People will absolutely care what you have to say, you just have to understand it may take years for you to find the right way to say it that resonates with your audience.

"I DON'T HAVE THE SKILLS REQUIRED TO MAKE MY IDEA HAPPEN."

I have virtually NO specific skills. I'm your quintessential jack-of-all-trades and a master of none. I dabble in design, but I'm years behind designers whose work actually receives praise and accolades. I don't know a thing about programming languages. I'm terrible at managing people. Really, one could argue that all I have are my ideas. But yet, I find ways to turn my ideas into realities. I seek out talented people to whom I can outsource my weaknesses. If you really want your ideas to happen, any skillset you might be lacking doesn't matter one bit. That's just a story you're telling yourself so you don't actually have to put in the work (or the risk) to make that thing you want to make. The only skills you really need are the work ethic and discipline to figure out how the heck you're going to get your idea out into the world. Someone else in the world knows what you don't. Find them. Pay them money. Exchange something for their time. No skills required.

"I CAN'T MAKE MONEY DOING WHAT I WANT TO DO."

Why not? Because other people haven't been able to? Those are *other people*; they aren't you. I'm never willing to accept assumptions based on the actions of others. You can make money doing literally anything right now thanks to the access afforded to us by the Internet.

I once wrote a silly joke in one of my Monday weekly email newsletters about becoming a professional snuggler. A few weeks later I received an email from a woman named Sam who started a Snuggling Agency (amazeballs) and has gone on to build a profitable snuggling business that's paid off her student loan debt and provided jobs (snuggling jobs!) for other people. Point taken.

I've made money doing weirdly outlandish things. My name has been included in segments on TV called "they get paid for that?" and "jobs you never thought you could get paid for." As the old adage goes, you won't know until you try. And as it relates to making money doing what you want to do, you absolutely won't know until you try (and try in all the different ways that other people haven't thought of before).

"I DON'T KNOW WHERE TO START."

By picking up this book, you are starting. By wanting to start, you are starting. So check that one off the list right now. But you know those things aren't enough. Eventually, you just have to put one foot in front of the other (or click a mouse one click in front of the other?). Start small, start scared, but just start.

***

Every one of these common excuses is based on some kind of assumption—some mental leap that you're taking in your own mind so you don't really have to put yourself out there and risk rejection. But remember, rejection comes with the territory. So listen to your own tired excuses that play in your mind and start calling yourself out. When you catch yourself in a thought that's trying to justify holding you back from what you really want to do or make, ask yourself: Is it a fact, or is it an assumption?

TEST ALL OF THE ASSUMPTIONS, ALL OF THE TIME

....

As I mentioned, there's no framework for getting better at testing your own assumptions. All you can do is make the commitment right now that the next time you catch yourself making an assumption, you'll take some kind of action to test it. This doesn't just go for your own assumptions either, this includes the assumptions of society, your friends, your family, etc., all of the time.

I don't assume that just because I read something in a book that it will work for me. I don't assume that because someone else does something a certain way I need to do it that way, too. I test those things. One by one. Assumption by assumption.

It's hard to be the tester of all the assumptions. Often times you run into people who don't like being questioned (I'm one of those people!). Like all things in life, you'll want to pick and choose your assumption-testing battles.

Here's one question that always helps me when I'm being met with an assumption: "Have I dealt with this exact issue before with the same exact circumstances?"

Almost always the answer is "No." It's nearly impossible for the answer to be "Yes," if only for the sheer fact that it's a different day, week, month, or year. (Unless you're a time traveler from the future and you're reliving this moment again. In that case, carry on. Also, do we finally have flying cars? I really want a flying car.) Acknowledging that the phrase "*I just know XYZ*" is actually an assumption disguised as a certainty changes everything. Sometimes it will feel like you're retesting assumptions you've already retested in a retest of assumption retesting before. (Head spinning yet?) Well, welcome to life and business. It's not a straight line. It winds like a looping roller coaster, and you'd better hold on for the ride.

IDEAS ARE NOTHING
WITHOUT EXECUTION

No idea has ever succeeded without execution. Every light bulb moment, "ah-ha!" brain explosion, and mad scientist that yelled "Eureka!" only happened after hours, days, weeks, months, and (often) years of work.

We all want success, but it's those of us who are willing to dive into the trenches who will find it. It's those of us who aren't afraid to make the necessary sacrifices that doing the hard work takes. Without doing the actual work, your ideas are nothing but fleeting thoughts. Testing your assumptions is taking action. It's stopping the endless loop of doubts and questions and presumptions in your head and starting the real work at hand: learning what will actually happen in the real world with your idea.

Assumptions are nothing more than fear-based fiction. Stop deciding what is probably going to happen and find out for real by doing it (while owning your weird, of course).

Chapter 6: "Own it!" recap and to-do item

- What assumption is holding you back? What limiting belief keeps swirling around in your head? Is this assumption or belief rooted in truth, or based on fear of the unknown or what you *think* might happen? Challenge this assumption by putting your weirdness out there and then reflect on the outcome. Remember, rejection is part of the journey, so if you experience some, wear it as a badge of honor and continue moving forward!

SECTION II

HOW I OWN MY WEIRD

Now that you know the basics of the Own Your Weird mindset, I want to share with you how I've applied these basic principles to my life and business the past few years. You'll see that I threw away the blueprint that existed for each area and learned to approach things through the lens of my uniqueness.

In redesigning each of these aspects of my life around my values and my own eccentricities, I get to actually enjoy each one on my own terms in a way that makes me happy. I hope the chapters in this section serve to (1) show you how to put these principles in action through a diverse range of topics and (2) remind you that with each area of your life—whether it's food and health, relationships, or social media—it's up to you to write the rules you live by.

CHAPTER 7

Social Media

I will warn you up front, the following chapter is going to make me sound like an old, cranky man. My relationship with social media over the years has undergone quite a transformation, and I will admit that some of the opinions I now have about it are not popular. But trust me when I say, my skepticism about social media is NOT just because I'm now entering my late thirties and it's time for me to pick up the obligatory distrust for technology and whatever "the kids" are into. I'm not going to go on a rant about millennials (can't we all just be people?!) or tell you why the robots are going to get us in the end (although I really think the aggressive nature of Roombas should at least give us all pause).

As someone whose entire business foundation once rested on constantly posting on social media for five years straight, I know firsthand what social media overuse can do to a person. I have no doubt that my reliance on social media and early heavy usage with IWearYourShirt have given me an ability to see some of the negative side effects of becoming overly absorbed in the digital world, which has no doubt shaped the way that I ultimately use social media differently than most people.

A SOCIAL MEDIA BILLBOARD?

My hyper-usage of social media started innocently enough in 2008 when I was a co-founder of a small design company. (For the sake of our timeline, this was after I finally got up the courage to leave my Beige Office of Mediocrity, but before I had the idea for IWearYourShirt.)

My job was "client relations and marketing," which essentially translates to "keep the clients happy." This is why, when I was on a random client call with one of our design clients, and he asked me what I knew about Facebook, I didn't answer with my immediate thought, which was, "I'm pretty sure that's just the place to scroll through people's baby photos or get into arguments about politics."

Instead, after a beat, I fired back: "What would you like to know?" (Any typical client relations person tries to pretend they know everything, even if they have no clue what they're talking about.)

The conversation that ensued had me wondering if Facebook and the other growing social media platforms like Twitter and YouTube could be viable channels to promote or market a business. Then, a funny thing happened. Another client asked a similar question. And a week later, another. Before I knew it, all of our design clients were asking me questions that related to social media.

Could Facebook be more than a place to get into arguments with your Uncle Gary about the current state of politics? (These are the big existential questions we all must ask ourselves.)

It was those early client conversations, mixed with thoughts I had been having about wanting to build my own unique business, that led to my big idea. I thought, *Why isn't there someone on social media who acts like a TV/radio/media spokesperson does?* There were millions of people already using these social media platforms. Could I be the first to step up and promote brands on social media like a walking, talking, T-shirt-wearing billboard?

Today the answer seems laughably obvious. Of course! "Influencer marketing" is an entire industry now, with brands happily paying eighteen-year-old YouTube stars thousands of dollars for one sponsored Instagram post. But at the time in 2008, this was a completely new concept—especially since most businesses were still largely under the impression that this whole social media thing was a fad.

The idea of being a social media spokesperson kept nagging at me, which is how the idea for IWearYourShirt was ultimately born. That, and looking at my closet one morning and realizing every T-shirt I owned had another company's name or logo on it, meaning I was paying *them* to promote *their* businesses. Nope—not on this crazy guy's watch! I knew there had to be a way for those companies to pay me.

POSTING LIKE IT WAS MY JOB (BECAUSE IT WAS)

When I finally dusted off that old Facebook account and got started posting with IWearYourShirt, it felt strange sharing my thoughts and feelings on my Facebook Wall (or was it my Timeline?—it's hard to keep track). I'm not naturally a real "share my feelings" kind of guy, and I especially wasn't back then. But I was committed to making this crazy social media/T-shirt idea work so I got over that weird feeling to post every single day, multiple times a day. I had to show the companies paying me that I had an audience and that I was interacting with people who would see their brand (even if it was just letting people know that I was going to Chick-Fil-A for lunch. #notasponsor #beforeIwasvegan).

Eventually, this is what literally filled my days. Every waking hour, I was either filming a YouTube video, editing a YouTube video, posting on Facebook, interacting with fans on Twitter, hosting a one-hour live video show, or commenting with people to grow the IWearYourShirt community. It became habitual and consuming. This wasn't about using social media in those in-between, standing-in-line-for-coffee, I-can't-stand-being-bored moments; this was a 24/7 full-time gig.

Looking back, there was always a part of me deep down that didn't love sharing every waking hour with other people. Sure, I liked the feeling of being entertaining, but it was overall exhausting. It's why even now when I see people glorify YouTubers who "get paid to be themselves," I don't envy them at all. I know the mental toll it can take when you feel compelled to share your entire life with an audience and when people feel they have ownership over your decisions. The lines between perception and reality get blurred, and I didn't know what to make of that. But, social media was literally paying my bills. I forced myself to rationalize all my time spent there because I saw it as a part of my overall goal of making my unique business succeed.

WHEN THE RULES CHANGE ON YOU

Near the end of the IWearYourShirt years, Facebook made a big change to their Pages algorithm. No longer were fans of your Page guaranteed to see your content. This was a move on Facebook's part to start making money through ads (great for you guys, Facebook), but for someone's business like mine that revolved entirely around engagement and interacting with content, it truly was a change of epic proportions.

Numbers started to drop dramatically. Posts on my Page went from getting hundreds of comments, likes, and shares to 10 percent of that interaction. I had to start explaining to clients why this was happening and why their sponsorship was still a great spend of their ad dollars. After pouring thousands of hours into growing my fan base on Facebook, I thought: *How could Facebook do this to me? How could they pull the rug out from under me like this? I've spent years promoting Facebook and building an audience there . . . what right do they have?!*

Okay, maybe a littttttttle dramatic . . . but this was my livelihood at the time. Facebook felt integral to the growth of my business and being able to get precious eyeballs on my shirts.

Years later, my good buddy Paul Jarvis wrote an article related to this very thing, titled "Whose Playground Are You Playing In?" This excerpt from Paul's article accurately sums up what I went through when Facebook made its big algorithm change:

> Every playground has its own rules, an owner, and a set of things you're allowed to do . . . In order to play in someone's playground you have to give them some of your power and energy. A bit of you now exists in a place where you don't have full control. Maybe it's agreeing that they can use anything you post in their own advertising (like Facebook). Maybe it's that your content can only exist in their system (like Instagram). Maybe in order to add something, you need to follow a strict set of rules (like Kickstarter). Sometimes the playground's owner takes their bouncy ball in the middle of a game and goes home forever (like Del.ico.us, Ping, Digg, Friendster, MySpace—they all closed shop and you can't play there anymore).
>
> There are pros to playing in other people's playgrounds. Sometimes

you can get more traction for what you create, sometimes they'll do a bit of promotion for you, and sometimes you can even become the star of the playground (like when folks get famous on YouTube).

But the problem, or downside, is always the same: it's not your playground and not your rules. They could always take their bouncy ball and go home in the middle of a game. You (and your revenue stream) could be banned from the jungle gym or monkey bars quickly, with anything from a terms and conditions update to a change in their revenue model (which excludes you making money).

It's true, Facebook had changed the rules of the game because they owned the playground. It was a wake-up call that taught me I wasn't fully in control of the trajectory of my business if it was fueled by social media. (Hello values, my old friend. Now I can see that this lack of control was part of my issue with social media.)

This, plus the personal toll that sharing everything was having on me, led to a major feeling of social media burnout. I found myself questioning everything about social media, from its addictive qualities, to what it was doing to human interaction, to the real impact it was (or wasn't) having on business success.

WHAT'S SOCIAL MEDIA DOING TO US?

YOUR PERFECTLY EDITED LIFE

Tell me you haven't taken a photo and then retaken it because you knew the first version was slightly blurry and people wouldn't "like" it. Tell me you haven't hit backspace on a thought, only to make it a more "likeable" thought to a larger group of people. Tell me you haven't been excited to share a moment or cool experience, only to decide none of your photos are good enough to do it justice so you opt to keep it to yourself.

I can guess you've done those things only because I'm guilty of doing them, too. In fact, I still find myself doing them. This instinct to share the perfectly edited version of life or to control the image we put out into the world stems from insecurities that have always been embedded deep within us—now we just have the tools that allow us to manipulate our lives in a way that minimizes those insecurities.

The most popular accounts on Instagram aren't people who share poorly cropped photos. The most popular accounts on YouTube don't feature 240p resolution videos with nearly inaudible sound. And the most popular moments of your life, as demonstrated to you by vanity metrics on the Internet, are only the most edited or exciting of the things you've shared. These are just facts.

But where does it end? Our real lives aren't perfectly edited. They're often messy and poorly lit and boring and awkward and all the things you rarely see on the highlight reels shared on social media.

Which has to make you wonder: if we're only ever sharing the "perfectly edited" versions of our lives, aren't we setting ourselves up for failure and disappointment when our reality doesn't match up? Are we further leading ourselves to disappear into our phones because "real life" just can't compare to the glossy magazine-and-movie-style content we're constantly seeing online? Social media and the Internet haven't been around long enough for us to understand the long-term effects of this emphasis on a perfectly edited life.

INSTANT GRATIFICATION JUNKIES

Right now I bet you can hear from ten to twenty people in a matter of seconds if you want to. You can hop on Twitter and ask a question. You can post a photo on Facebook for comments (I don't know much these days, but I'm betting baby photos still get all the interaction). You can snap or story something on your phone. You can check your email. You can do all these things and get an immediate response and the instant gratification of connecting with someone else.

What's the result? Look around the next time you're in a public place. Look for someone on their phone (they won't be hard to find). Turn your head slightly, squint your eyes, and ask yourself: "Does that person look like some kind of drugged-out zombie?" Keep an eye out for the tell-tale signs: slumped shoulders, mouth open, eyes glazed over, and usually complete and utter obliviousness to whatever is going on around them. (Caroline and I call the slumped shoulders/head down, staring at a screen look "low-power mode." How many humans can you spot in low-power mode in just ten seconds?)

Being sucked into our electronic devices is not the same as being sucked into a book, TV, movies, the newspaper, etc. (Note: these are ancient relics that still exist as of writing this book.) There's an all-consuming-ness to having a supercomputer at your fingertips with an endless supply of information—or what's more enticing, an endless supply of validation and gratification from other humans if you need it. It takes mental effort to put our devices down or set them in another room, and it's a feat of personal restraint to not refresh or swipe for new notifications and posts. And the worst part? We start to actually believe that the approval of strangers is what matters in our lives.

Don't get me wrong, my life is unarguably better because of technology, social media, and electronic devices. What I'm saying is, there's a cost. And the majority of people aren't self-aware enough to see the zombies they are becoming.

Once I started realizing I was burned out on social media, it's like I started to see the world through a new pair of glasses. Everywhere I turned I found a family of four sitting at a restaurant in silence on their devices, or a couple on a date, finger-swiping their way through perfectly edited lives of other people—not the real human being sitting in front of them. I'd see a friend trying to subtly (or not so subtly) reply to a text mid-conversation at dinner or almost run into a stranger on the sidewalk whose eyes were glued to their screen.

I'm not trying to come off like a curmudgeon or shake my cane at you (because I can't, I need it for my balance and my bad back). I'm just trying to share with you the observations that became so painfully clear to me after I stopped allowing myself to be a technology zombie and started paying attention.

MY FIRST SOCIAL MEDIA DETOX

When IWearYourShirt closed down in 2013, I have to admit a part of me was relieved because I no longer felt beholden to Facebook or Twitter or YouTube. I could finally hit reset and draw new boundaries with social media.

Unfortunately, as I was trying to figure out what my next business move would be, the world had changed its opinion about social media. No longer was it being viewed as an online fad. People were starting to see that it was the evolution of the Internet itself and it wasn't going anywhere. Of course, online business owners and marketers wasted no time in figuring out how to use this to their advantage. Everywhere I looked people were recommending the use of Facebook Pages and Facebook Ads to promote their businesses. People swore this was the only way to get traffic to a blog or website now. But I wanted to test this assumption.

The wool had already been pulled back from my eyes and I was starting to see social media in my life and others' lives for what it was: a dependency. I knew I was using social media as a crutch, thanks to an endless supply of instant gratification. When I was afraid to work on something hard or challenging, I'd escape to checking tweets and my FB feed. While writing articles for my website, I felt the strong urge to check the little red notifications on my social media sites (damn you, browser tabs!).

I also noticed unwanted changes in my mindset. I found myself becoming more cynical and comparing myself to other people. I'd see a fellow online business owner pop up in my feed promoting a product or service, and I'd feel jealousy or anger toward them. I try to preach putting more positivity out into the world, but every time I would check a feed of updates, I felt negativity creeping in.

So, I decided to do an experiment: a thirty-day detox from social media. Sounds pretty weird, right? I knew what it felt like to have social media at my fingertips; what would it feel like when it was taken away? Would my business take a downturn (at this point my income relied heavily on blog traffic and course sales)? Would I feel sad and disconnected? What the heck would I spend all that extra time on? These were the questions I wanted to answer. So, I used an app called Self Control to block myself from any social sites for a month, I removed all social media apps from my phone (FB, Twitter, Instagram, and YouTube) and I wrote a daily journal about the experience. Funny enough, since my first social media detox our smartphones now have app-blocking controls built directly into the operating systems. Seems big companies are taking notice and trying to do something to help users take back some of their attention and focus.

The result of my social media detox? While the first seven to ten days were tough (I truly did feel like a junkie who desperately needed my fix), my productivity, attention span, and clarity of thought all increased greatly by living without social media for a month. I felt like I broke bad habits (refreshing feeds and checking notifications) in a very short period of time. I didn't have some crazy epiphany and move to a remote cabin in the woods after that. Instead, the mindfulness that my thirty-day detox created became a snowball that gradually picked up steam over time. After that first experiment, I kept the Facebook, Twitter, and YouTube apps off my phone. I stopped focusing any attention on filtering my posts/thoughts or even sharing blog posts on social media at all.

The one radical leap I did take, though, was on Facebook. These little baby steps were just prolonging what I already knew deep in my gut: it was time to quit

Facebook. (This was the one site that I genuinely felt was bringing only negativity into my life.) So, finally, in 2016, I wrote Facebook a breakup post:

Facebook, it's time we took a break.

We've been together for over 12 years. Kind of hard to believe, right?

I remember when it was just you, me, "the wall," a few silly pokes, and a couple friends sharing tidbits about our lives. It was innocent. You were trying to figure yourself out, and I was in my 20s trying to do the same.

But, my oh my, times have changed, haven't they? And I'm not naive enough to think things would always be the same as they were in the beginning.

One thing I've learned about our relationship over the years is that you're kind of demanding, Facebook. Actually, that's not true. You're extremely demanding. I know that won't offend you because that's who you are and who you've always been. And anyway, that worked for me in the beginning because I was young and trying to learn about myself and what mattered to me.

But you see, I've changed.

I didn't realize it up until a few years ago, but I'm actually kind of introverted. Which is why I think I felt so comfortable being in a relationship with you and using you as a conduit to reach so many other interesting people. You did a great job of that. You helped open up doors for my life (and business) that may have never existed. I really do appreciate and thank you for that.

But I've had one big realization about our relationship, and it's probably due to my growing older and having more life experience: I don't enjoy sharing every detail of my life with you anymore. I don't like the way you make me feel—like I have to scream for attention every time I have something to say.

You've probably noticed I've been acting differently too. I'm not signed in to you on a daily basis. I don't have your chat turned on, nor do I check your messages. I deleted your app from my phone a couple of years ago. And recently, I installed a plugin on my browser that blocked your News Feed altogether. I've slowly been pulling away from you and limiting how much you can grasp my attention.

But there's another thing: I feel like a better person when I'm not with you.

You see, we've taken a couple short breaks from each other over the past couple years. Four of them, in fact. If I reflect on those times apart, they're the times when I've felt the most creative and most unencumbered to make things and experience the life I've tried to build for myself. Notice I didn't say "share the life . . . "

Sharing my life with you has been a rollercoaster ride, Facebook. My biggest accomplishments receive praise and cheers from people all around the world. My failures, mistakes, and normal life experiences get swept under the timeline rug, leaving me feeling empty.

Without you, I wouldn't know what dopamine was or how interacting with you gives my brain the same chemical response as doing cocaine.[1] To be honest, that fucking scares me, Facebook. And the worst part? Since 2005, you've done everything in your power to increase my dopamine responses while using you. You've introduced more ways to Like something, to peer in on others. And you're so damn intelligent these days that I'll catch myself sucked into viewing the cascading timeline of other people's lives, not realizing how much time I've wasted scrolling through moments that you convinced other people to share. Before my first self-imposed social media detox, for example, I would scroll through your News Feed for hours and leave you open in a browser tab all day long. I could never stop being with you.

I used to really enjoy being with you and all my other friends in one place. There was a time when there were no agendas to being with you. It was fun to see where friends would travel to and reconnect with people I'd lost touch with over the years.

No one cared about the "right" time to drop a little update about their lives.

No one took 14 different versions of a photo just to try to find "the one" that would get the most Likes/shares/comments (aka dopamine responses).

---

1   "Are Facebook Likes Similar to Cocaine Addiction?," Skeptics Stack Exchange, https://skeptics.stackexchange.com/questions/22207/are-facebook-likes-similar-to-cocaine-addiction.

No one was trying to milk every ounce of you to feel as good about themselves or their businesses as possible.

No one was sharing their opinions just to join in the cycle of everyone sharing their opinions.

I know that being on you is a game, Facebook—a game I could win if I wanted to. I could write posts with words of reflection and inspiration, accompanied by a share-worthy photo. I could jump on every intriguing world topic and weigh in with my thoughts, perspective, and wit. Heck, I could even outsource my use of you to someone more well-equipped to handle your demands.

But all those things would keep me hooked on you. Hooked on you, Facebook, like a junkie hooked on a drug.

I'm one of the fortunate ones. I feel my deep emotional attachment to you and know we've been on a slippery slope together. An uncharted slope, without decades of research and studies to prove what I feel in my heart. Somehow, you've wooed 58% of the US population into hanging out with you every day, and I just don't want to be one of your guinea pigs anymore.

You are the next great addiction, Facebook. And I want to quit you.

This is me, closing the door on our relationship. I'm not slamming it shut, locking it, and throwing away the key. I'm simply shutting the door gently and walking away. Maybe I'll be back if I realize my life was better off with you in it. But I'm going to put this feeling of a necessary separation to the test.

I know you won't miss me, as I'm but one small twinkling star in your vast solar system of galaxies, planets, and much brighter stars. Tomorrow, you and everyone reading this will have moved on to some other moment in someone else's timeline.

Thank you for everything you've done for me since 2005.

I know, I know. So dramatic, ha! I originally intended that letter to be my final comic commentary on how I believed Facebook was a toxic force in my life, but after reading it again, it comes off more poignant for me than comical.

Ultimately it just comes down to this one line in the letter: "I feel like a better person when I'm not with you." I'm definitely a more positive, more productive, more conscientious human being when I'm not spending all my waking hours scouring a news feed, and I don't think I would have made that discovery without trying a social media detox.

(By the way, as of writing this book, the term "social media detox" is the Google search that is the single largest contributor in traffic to my website, to the tune of nearly three hundred thousand website visitors in two years! Clearly I'm not the only one that has woken up to the negative side effects of social media and is curious about what life might look like with a little less connectivity.)

THE NEXT GREAT ADDICTION

You may not know what it feels like to be separated from Facebook. You may be reading this and thinking to yourself: "I don't need a social media detox. The way I use Facebook is fine." But before you have a knee-jerk reaction, I'd like to challenge you to test the assumption that your use of Facebook and how it makes you feel (and act) is, actually, fine.

Having publicly shared my thoughts while doing social media detoxes, I've heard the following from people when I challenge them to take a break from Facebook (or any social platform):

"I don't need to take a break."

"I'm in full control of how I use Facebook. It doesn't control me."

"I could quit at any time, I just choose not to."

Do me a favor? Reread those reactions and put them in the context of drug/alcohol use. They're the exact same objections. When you're addicted to something, as I believe we all are (to some degree) with social media sites, you're blind to the fact that a problem exists.

I believe social media, and Facebook especially, is the next great drug addiction. If you can't turn something off, if you can't leave it alone for days, if you feel an incredibly powerful urge to constantly be checking notifications . . . you are addicted.

And you are NOT alone. I was right there with you.

Kristen Lindquist, professor of psychology at the University of North Carolina, Chapel Hill, says social information feels intrinsically rewarding to people. We get a jolt of dopamine when someone "likes" our Facebook post or retweets our Twitter link. Over time, the effect on the reward center in the brain is similar to what makes drug addicts go back for another line of cocaine.

The problem with social media—and I'm sure I'm coming off like a hemp-sandal-wearing hippie who makes his own grain-free granola for saying it this way—is that it's all so *new*. We don't have any long-term studies or data to understand the effect it is having on us and our lives. I'm not a scientist, and odds are you probably aren't either, but can't you agree that it's just worth taking some time to figure out how using something like Facebook every day impacts you and your life?

One of the objections I hear when I challenge people to take a break from Facebook (or other social platforms) is some version of this: but how will I keep up with my friends and family?

Remember how social media sites didn't exist ten-ish years ago? Remember how you still had family members and friends back then? And somehow, through the miraculous-ness that is technology, you were able to stay in touch and "keep up?"

I'm not advocating that everyone needs to immediately quit Facebook. What I am advocating is taking a break. Give yourself a chance to see what your life feels like when you remove Facebook (or Twitter, Instagram, Snapchat, et al.) from the equation. You might find out who your true friends really are. You might realize how much better you feel each day not having everyone else's agendas or opinions pushed in your face. You might even find all that elusive time you've been searching for to work on your business, idea, or to improve the actual relationships in your life.

HOW IT FEELS TO LET GO

I'll be the first one to tell you, changing your social media habits and disrupting your dopamine dependency isn't easy. In fact, leaving Facebook might have ended up being the easiest part for me. What ended up being a lot harder was walking away from "the numbers" and the notoriety that I had accumulated with IWearYourShirt. I want to share these stories with you because I think they illustrate just how much we come to derive our identity and confidence from our social media personas—and the vanity metrics that accompany them.

WALKING AWAY FROM FIFTEEN MILLION-PLUS VIEWS ON YOUTUBE

When I walked away from my IWearYourShirt (IWYS) business in 2013, I also walked away from a thriving YouTube channel. I wasn't getting the same viewership on my daily videos as I had in the IWYS heydays of 2009/2010, but I was still averaging five hundred to a thousand views the day after uploading a video. And in total, with thirty-three hundred–plus videos on that YouTube channel, I had amassed over fifteen million views. (And no, that isn't a typo . . . that's fifteen million views.) This is six years before the rise of Casey Neistat and the explosion of daily vlogging, so at the time that number was a rarity and something I was immensely proud of. Of the thirty-three hundred videos on the IWearYourShirt channel, I had personally created nearly seventeen hundred. (That's a shirt-load of videos!)

When I closed IWearYourShirt, I wondered if I should do something else with the YouTube channel and all the viewership it had attached to it. I thought about selling my YouTube channel. Certainly that would have been weird, right? Had I done that, though, I would have lost all control of the thousands of hours of effort / and those hours had my face plastered all over them (it wouldn't be like selling an app or website, where your identity isn't closely tied to it).

What I realized about my "thriving" YouTube channel was that it was only thriving in the sense that it was generating wonderful vanity metrics. When I was shutting down IWearYourShirt, these vanity metrics weren't helping me pay my mortgage, lose the excess weight I'd gained, or remove stress from my life. The more I thought about allowing my self-worth to be defined by views on videos, the more I realized those numbers were strangling my creativity. Once I realized my YouTube channel (and the views that came with it) weren't actually providing value to my life and business any longer, the decision to walk away from my channel became much easier. I also knew that creating YouTube videos took about six to eight hours per day, hours that I could get back and invest in creating something new (something to help me course-correct my life/business ship).

BECOMING THE FIRST UN-VERIFIED USER ON TWITTER

One random morning in August 2012, I received an email letting me know I had become a Verified account on Twitter. To me, this officially meant I had "made it"—I'd joined the ranks of the Kardashians, professional athletes, politicians, and @charmin (yep, that's verified toilet paper—the good stuff).

When I logged in to my Twitter account that day, I was greeted with a fancy little blue icon with a check mark in it next to my (previous) username, @iwearyourshirt. Talk about validation! My day in the sun was upon me. No longer would I have to do my own laundry! (Spoiler alert: getting verified on Twitter doesn't mean you no longer have to do your laundry. In fact, as I would soon learn, it doesn't mean much of anything.)

Like any other normal person on planet Earth, it felt really good to be noticed by Twitter and to become a Verified account. A few years later, Twitter started letting people apply to be Verified, but I feel strangely proud that I was chosen, like the little green alien toys in the Toy Story movies (the claaaawwwww!). Because I was chosen, I held on to my Verified status and clutched it tightly like a small child with a stuffed animal.

Years after being Twitter-chosen, although still having to wash and fold my own laundry (ugh), I had stopped using the moniker "IWearYourShirt" on every other platform, social media channel, and day-to-day business site because the business had officially shut down. But, if you change your Twitter username, you lose your verified status. Thus, the last remaining piece of the IWearYourShirt puzzle to put back in the box was my Twitter username.

Now it might sound silly to you, but this decision—finally changing my @IWearYourShirt username and thus losing my verified status—was harder than I'd like to admit. When you come up with an idea that truly represents own- ing your weird, and you fight through the rejection and the ridicule, and you come out on the other side with some measure of acceptance and validation, you want to do everything in your power to hold onto it. The little blue check mark felt like a thumbs-up from the world saying "You did something unique and it paid off." Some days I'd find myself staring at my own Twitter profile, trying to envision what it would be like without that life-affirming little check mark. (I may have even Photoshopped my own Twitter profile to NOT have the Verified badge on it as a way to ease into the unverified realm. Let's just say that was a low point in my mental battles over letting something so meaningless define a part of my life.)

After weeks of being on the fence, my friend Jeff Sheldon from Ugmonk finally gave me the tiny nudge I was looking for when he DM'd me one day. He said: "Random, but have you thought about changing your Twitter handle? Or is there still value from the IWYS days? I feel like you're more than just that."

He was 1,000 percent right, if that's even possible. I, as a human person, was way more than just IWearYourShirt. Not only had I gone on to do a bunch of weird and unique projects since then, but as people we are so much more than what we do and what we achieve. I needed to let go and move on.

I navigated to my settings page, typed in my new username (@jasondoesstuff because . . . I do a lot of stuff), and clicked the confirmation message acknowledging I would be losing the tiny blue check mark, the thought of which gave me so much consternation.

I sat there in front of my laptop, still feeling the sting of ripping off the band-aid, and I remember Caroline walked in the room and said, "Trust me, in a week you won't even care."

And she was right.

Am I really going to let some stupid small blue icon next to my name on Twitter define who I am and dictate how I feel about myself? No. I'm not. Not anymore.

(As a side note, all of my Twitter followers did not magically disappear after I became unverified. People did not immediately cast me aside and stop talking to me on Twitter. In fact, I probably get way less Twitter Spam now that I'm unverified.)

It feels ridiculous to type these next words, but that decision to unverify my Twitter account was one of the hardest decisions I had made in my life, which further proves my point of the hold that social media has on us. We're all met with these virtual challenges that never existed a decade ago. We're constantly struggling with the "what ifs" of social media, which is why I so strongly believe we have to control how we use these platforms and not let their (insanely powerful) algorithms control us.

Our number of followers or our arbitrary popularity status on some website doesn't define who we are as actual people. Finally decoupling my identity from something I'd spent years placing way too much stock in gave me a sense of freedom; I felt like I was taking back control.

It's worth taking the time to ask yourself: would you grapple with the decision to deactivate one of your social media accounts? Would you cling to your own verified badge—or whatever arbitrary digital symbol brings you validation? Would you think twice before walking away from a YouTube channel with millions of views? If you know the answer is yes, it's worth examining the kind of hold these sites have on you. It's worth remembering that you are so much more than a follower count, a VIP designation, or a channel persona. You're a human being. Don't ever forget that.

YOUR BUSINESS CAN SUCCEED
WITHOUT FACEBOOK

Now I'm sure the big question you're wondering is, did my move away from Facebook and my scaling back on social media affect my business? I'll skip to the punch line: YES—but not in the way you're probably assuming.

When I wrote and shared my final goodbye letter to Facebook in late 2016, it came with some internal struggle. Would my business continue to make money if I wasn't posting regular updates and racking up followers?

Well, I'll let the numbers speak for themselves. In 2016 (the year I quit Facebook), my business made more money than ever before in my life, with less than 4 percent of the website traffic to all of my sites coming from social media (less than 2 percent coming from Facebook specifically). To put that into undeniably clear numbers for you:

- In 2015, my site JasonDoesStuff.com had 157,000 unique visitors. Less than 3,800 of those came from Facebook (2.4 percent). Total revenue that year (which is fueled almost entirely by my email list and website traffic) was $214,000.

- In 2016, the year I quit Facebook and scaled way back on social media, JasonDoesStuff.com had 327,000 unique visitors. Less than 5,600 of those came from Facebook (1.7 percent). Revenue that year rose to $280,000.

These low referral percentages are obviously due to the fact that I wasn't posting or focusing on social media, but the more important thing I want you to take away from those numbers is that my business actually started doing better when I was no longer paying attention to social media.

Now you might be asking yourself what did I do instead? For one, I started writing a lot more. I made sure the intention of every article began with the phrase: "I want to help you . . . "

Rarely when we post anything to social media is it about helping the person on the other end. So often it feels like "Look what I'm doing" rather than "Look what I can do for you." But with the weekly articles I enjoyed writing, I now had a filter to make sure the content I was creating would be useful. I started sharing lessons and actionable advice on things I had experience with like writing sales copy, establishing core values, understanding the importance of email marketing (where I make 98 percent of my income), and the overwhelming benefits of social media detoxes. (Pro tip: writing useful content also makes it much more likely that someone searching for help on a topic will find your content, opt-in for more of it, and ultimately pay you money so you can continue to be helpful.)

I had all this freed-up time thanks to not scrolling or posting on social media—time that I also utilized to make online courses with other creative people. These online courses were about everything from finishing your (damn) book to podcasting like a boss, to developing a unique/kickass personal brand. Better yet, I had the time to actually respond to my customers and keep up with them. I was able to go above and beyond to provide excellent customer service and really devote time to helping my customers succeed. These were the things that really moved the needle for me. The amount of mental energy I had recovered proved invaluable for the growth of my business and for my day-to-day happiness.

So the truth is, YES, walking away from social media did affect my business—it affected it in a positive way. I was able to develop a business strategy that put me in control: writing articles about things I had real experience in, optimizing them for what people were searching for (SEO), building an engaged email list of subscribers, delivering value to those subscribers on a consistent basis, and converting a percentage of those subscribers into paying customers of my courses and software products. And all of those things I did in my own weird way! Nowadays, I enjoy showing up in someone's email inbox where I don't have to worry about them scrolling right past me, looking for the next perfectly edited moment of someone else's life.

Chapter 7: "Own it!" recap and to-do item

- I present to you . . . A social media detox challenge. Can you do it? Can you take a break from ALL social media sites for a weekend, a full week, or *gasp* an entire month? I've challenged thousands of people around the world to do this and I've never had a single person say it wasn't impactful for them to take a break. So, what'll it be? How long can you take your first social media detox for?

CHAPTER 8

Debt and Money

This is the part of this book where we dig in deep with something I consider to be a failure (getting into over $100,000 in debt) and where I tell you the story of how I pulled myself up by my bootstraps and figured a way out. Many authors who write books like this one will paint a very pretty picture for you. A picture with barely any mistakes, blemishes, or holy-hell-Batman-this-ship-is-sinking moments. Not this book. Strap yourself in for the ride; it's about to get real.

First, can we all just admit we've dealt with debt? Some of us are magical wizards and have only had a couple thousand dollars in debt (if you've never even had that much, you are a Level 13 Wizard, with mystical powers beyond comprehension). But the majority of us have dealt with amounts of debt that have left us feeling shame, guilt, embarrassment, anger, confusion, and my personal favorite, there's-no-hope-in-the-world-I'll-ever-get-out-of-this-debt (or a feeling I affectionately named TNHITWIEGOOTD. Yep, TNHITWIEGOOTD is a real feeling, my friend).

In 2013, the debt number that was staring me in the face was $124,094. The number has not been embellished for dramatic effect. That was real, honest-to-grossness, debt. (So yeah, if there's a dollar amount that warrants that TNHITWIEGOOTD feeling, it's a six-figure one.) For more context, here's how that debt was broken down:

- My business debt (from IWearYourShirt): $72,328

- Caroline's business debt: $6,764

- Caroline's student loans: $20,208

- Volkswagen Tiguan lease payoff: $24,794

- Total debt: $124,094

To say that $124,094 in debt felt crippling would be an understatement. Being in debt feels like you're trapped on a motorized hamster wheel perpetually stuck in ON mode. Around and around you go with no end in sight, feeling like a furry little rodent who will never be able to step off the wheel and take a rest.

That feeling alone would be bad enough, but then, as you know, there are the . . . (dun dun DUN!) interest fees. Interest fees are like being stuck in a hole and for every inch you dig yourself out, the bottom of the hole drops six inches deeper. Interest fees make it feel like the game is unbeatable. I share this with you to make sure you know I understand how helpless and overwhelmed debt can make you feel.

The worst part for me was the $72,328 in business debt. Not only was I crushed by the sheer size of the amount, but I also resented this debt. I loathed this debt. With all of my being, I wanted to believe this debt didn't exist.

It's one thing for debt to come from a school loan, car loan, or an epic Black Friday splurge at Bloomingdale's. (Because, obviously, Bloomingdale's.) You can see where the debt came from. You can acknowledge that you were at fault for overspending, but that it got you something tangible that you were willing to rack up debt for.

Business debt is different—especially business debt for a business that no longer exists. That. Just. Plain. Hurts. You're paying for (or attempting with all your hamster-wheel-effort to pay for) mistakes you made or risks you took or decisions that didn't pan out. When the business is defunct, every dollar laughs at you in your face like a creepy, sadistic-looking circus clown. At least it did for me.

What can you do, though? Pretend it doesn't exist? Tuck it away in a corner and hope you hit the lotto so you can finally pay it off? Not a good plan. Once I finally came to the conclusion that I was the only one who could dig myself out of this hole, slowly but surely, I started to feel a tiny bit of power come back to me. There was one important realization I came to after stewing for months about my debt, which was: **I didn't get into debt overnight, and I couldn't expect to get *out* of debt overnight.**

I'm not sure why this thought was what triggered the light bulb moment for me, but nonetheless, the light bulb flashed ON. Almost immediately, it shifted my perspective from seeing my debt as something I had to pay off as soon as possible—something that felt impossible and overwhelming to accomplish—to seeing my debt as a long game I would continue to play, with levels upon levels I would have to conquer gradually.

This realization was timed well with my discovery of the book *The Obstacle Is the Way.* My debt, much like my business failure, was just another obstacle that I could use as an opportunity to teach me something. As much as I hated to admit it, $124,094 in debt was better than 2x, 5x, or 10x that amount. I had read stories, like we all have, of entrepreneurs and business owners who had to file bankruptcy and flip their entire lives upside down because of their debt. I didn't have to do those things, and that was something I could be grateful for. This helped me start to see my debt and our money challenges differently, and start coming up with a plan to tackle it.

DEBT AS A GAME

In devising our debt payoff plan, I asked myself if there was a unique way I could approach our unfortunate money situation. How could I see this problem through my own weird lens and make it more manageable? That's when I realized I had to start seeing debt as a game to be won. Rather than being ashamed or resentful of the position I was in, the competitive part of me started seeing it as a challenge. Could I whittle this huge sum of money down to nothing? I wanted to find out.

The first basic thing I came to understand was, there are two ways to get out of debt: Make more money or spend less money. (And if you can do a combination of both, your debt will get paid off faster.) Welp, that's it, secret's out—you're welcome! Thanks for reading my story about debt. Oh, what's that? I have to keep going? It's not that simple? Okay, got it. Well then let me be a little more specific about how we slayed our Debt Monster.

STRATEGY #1: SPEND LESS MONEY

GETTING ORGANIZED (AND OUT OF DENIAL)

It's true what they say, you know—the first step to recovery is admitting you have a problem. I've found this definitely applies to money as well. Money challenges, and debt specifically, can be a source of shame for a lot of people. The way many people choose to deal with this is by simply not checking their balances or refusing to look at their finances at all. Living in this state of denial feels better in the short run because you don't have to confront your problems, but all it ends up doing is multiplying in the long run. You start berating yourself for not tackling it sooner or it just gets worse and worse as your credit card balance grows in the shadows.

I knew the very first thing we had to do was rip off the Band-Aid. Step one was pulling up all of our accounts and actually coming up with a final tally, one number that we could stare in the face. If our debt was a game to win, our number was like the video game boss we finally knew we had to beat.

To beat our Debt Monster, we knew it wasn't enough to face our total sum of debt—we also needed to confront our spending habits (something we had never done). Caroline and I sat down and made a spreadsheet cataloging every single item we'd spent money on for the past ninety days. Once we wrote out all our expenses (yes every single one, including the $2.33 we spent at CVS on Q-tips and a snack-sized bag of Cool Ranch Doritos) . . . we were shocked. We were spending a lot more money than we thought we were. Now that we live in an age of credit cards, money can seem like it just turns into a series of numbers showing up on a website. The numbers are always changing, with money always coming in and going out, and it can be really easy to get desensitized to seeing those numbers or having a real understanding of what's going out.

MINIMIZING EXPENSES

After we got done writing out all of our expenses, I noticed a few places where we could save money. Once I added it up, I was astonished with how much money we could save on a yearly basis without even making big sacrifices to our daily lifestyle. Here are a few I identified right away:

- **Cell phone bill (Yearly savings: $1,440)**—We were paying $260/month for a family plan. I went into AT&T and asked them if they had a better option based on my usage. They did, and I brought our plan down to $140/month.

- **Cable bill (Yearly savings: $600)**—We were paying $185/month and hadn't changed our cable plan in years. I called and asked for a better plan and although it took a while, I was able to reduce my rate to $135/month. (Since the initial look at our expenses, we've officially become cable cutters, now saving us an additional $1,620/year. Turns out life doesn't end when you no longer have hundreds of channels to choose from.)

- **Food (Yearly savings: $6,000)**—We were paying $2,000ish/month on food (with $1,400 of that being eating out). This is partially because we're foodies and we viewed eating out as an experience we truly enjoyed and a way to connect. But we realized this number was high because without a real plan for buying groceries and cooking meals, we often deferred to going out, which racked up our food total big time. We definitely needed a budget, so we started with a manageable change to spend only $1,500/month on food (half for eating out, half for groceries). When we ran out of money for eating out, we couldn't eat out again until the next month.

- **Entertainment (Yearly savings: $1,800)**—Between drinks with friends, seeing movies (another favorite hobby of ours), two Netflix subscriptions in one house (unnecessary), and a bunch of other stuff, we realized we were overspending here. Writing all this out showed me we could cut back and save over $150 per month.

Just by taking a hard look at our biggest monthly expenses and being willing to make a few phone calls (or store walk-ins), we were able to find nearly $10,000 we could reallocate to our debt in the next twelve months. That's without making a single dollar extra or radically changing our lifestyle. I don't know about you, but I'm fairly certain you don't have $10,000 lying around to put toward your debt. We didn't think we did either, until we actually looked.

MAKING THE TOUGH PHONE CALLS

Once we made some small changes to our habits, the next step for our "spending less money" Debt Monster strategy was to stop the hemorrhaging from the interest fees and get our credit card totals back under control.

Did you know that most credit card companies have what's called a "hardship case?" It's a standard offering that most credit card companies can institute, but for reasons that will become clear in a moment, they never advertise.

What credit card companies want to avoid like the plague is people defaulting on their credit cards completely. They would much rather you keep paying down your debt, even if they make a little less interest on your payments, because they still want to collect on that debt you've racked up. This is where the "hardship case" comes in.

After writing out all of our expenses, we looked at our monthly credit card payments. I dug into those payments and looked closer at the APR (Annual Percentage Rate). That 0 percent APR we all pay (commence humongous eye roll at Jennifer Garner and Samuel L. Jackson) doesn't last forever. The APR on my American Express business card had climbed to 24 percent. Youch. I knew my APR wasn't 0 percent, but I had no idea it was that high. I decided to just pick up the phone and call American Express to see what my options were and if they could help. I'd been a loyal cardholder for five-plus years and had never missed a monthly payment. Maybe, just maybe, if I asked nicely, they'd reduce my APR by 1 to 5 percent? There was only one way to find out.

I navigated the endless phone tree, sat on hold listening to some contemporary jazz, and finally got to a real human person. I was completely honest with this fellow carbon-based life-form and explained my situation. I told him that:

- My business had gone under, leaving me with a maxed out credit card

- I didn't have any solid income in the foreseeable future

- I was worried I might miss my next payment or two

- I had no idea my APR had gotten so high

- I was scared I might have to default on the debt owed

That's the moment I learned about a "hardship case." He informed me that American Express would lower my credit card APR to 0 percent for three months, 1 percent for the following three months, and then 9.99 percent for the six months following that. Yes, they would freeze my card during that time, but I was already resigned to never using my card anyway (a $0.00 available credit balance isn't really helpful anyway.)

Finding out that American Express offered this option, I took to the phone again and called Citi Card and Wells Fargo (where I had other cards). They didn't have the same type of hardship case as AMEX, but they did offer to lower my APR.

Now, I will admit these were incredibly hard calls to make. They were humbling. I had to talk to multiple people in some cases to finally get up the chain and get what I needed, but all-in I spent about an hour on the phone. One hour that would save me over $400 in credit card fees each month?! That's an additional $4,800 a year, which—when you add in the savings from my expense-reassessment—meant I had nearly $15,000 to pay down my debt in the next year. Plus, no longer did it feel like that hole was getting six inches deeper for every one inch I dug out. Getting those interest fees under control was the first step to building momentum and really feeling I could take control back into my hands.

MOVE YOUR MONEY TO OTHER CREDIT CARDS

You may end up calling your existing credit card companies and not getting amazing results. That's okay! Not everyone (or every card company) is going to be helpful. But there's more than one way to beat the Debt Monster.

Another strategy that came in handy for us was a balance transfer. Basically this means applying for other credit cards, asking for the highest line of credit you can get, then doing 0 percent balance transfers. This gets tricky, but bear with me. This is probably best explained by walking you through the steps I took:

- In 2013, I found the Discover It credit card had the best balance transfer option available (thank you, NerdWallet.com).

- I applied for the card (yes, while having $124,094 in debt).

- I got approved and with a $5,000 limit! Amazing how this happens when you have "good credit" (don't even get me started on the complete fallacy of the idea of a credit score).

- I called Discover and asked for the highest credit limit possible. They said: "How much would you like?" I said $20,000. They said "No sir, how about $12,000?" I said, "Let's do it!"

- I transferred $12,000 from another credit card (my Wells Fargo card, the one with the highest APR) for a one-time fee of $363.

- I now had twelve months with 0 percent APR on this new card to pay down $12,000 that was previously costing me 18 percent APR.

- I cut up the old card (Wells Fargo) and left the account dormant with autopay turned on (just in case random expenses that I forgot about hit the card).

I repeated this with Chase and used the Chase Slate card to move debt from two other cards. This process doesn't work for everyone, but if you have good credit you can almost always keep getting credit cards. The key here is REALLY important: just remember you're not using them for spending! This level of the Debt Monster game is about getting your interest rates as low as absolutely possible on your existing debt (and, of course, to stop racking up more debt).

"THE SNOWBALL EFFECT"

Dave Ramsey has a term called the "Snowball Effect" that advises that you pay off your smallest debt with the highest interest rate first. Your first instinct might be to tackle the highest credit card balance first, but that doesn't give you momentum. It doesn't create the "snowball effect" of seeing debt disappear and being able to make noticeable progress.

I can tell you from experience that when we paid off our smallest credit card (which had $1,500 on it), it felt incredibly empowering. Yeah, we still had $122,000 in debt to get rid of, but that sense of completion and power from paying off one card gave us the motivation we needed to keep going. After a few months of making changes and having those hard phone calls, it was a tiny milestone that made us feel like it was all going to be worth it. It made us drunk with debt-payoff power (one of the best, and safest, types of drunk you can be!).

SPENDING LESS MONEY: A MINDSET SHIFT

Creating a plan to slay the Debt Monster is as much about the sacrifices in spending you make as it is about the shift you make in your mentality. You don't have to feel restricted or spend less forever (although you may just find that it inspires a more lasting, minimal lifestyle like it did with us). If it's an easier pill to swallow, learn to look at it as a temporary change.

We set a goal of paying off our $124,094 in debt in two to four years. Aggressive? Yes. But that's how we roll. We shifted our mindset from thinking we'd be living a life of sacrifice forever to realizing we'd be living a life of abundance (and way less stress) once we were debt-free.

Would it suck to not see as many movies in the theater while scarfing down a Combo #1 from the concession stand? It would. Would it feel limiting to question every purchase we made? Sure. But in a few years, when we'd put in the hard work, we could enjoy some of our favorite indulgences that much more knowing they weren't sinking us deeper into a hole we couldn't get out of.

High-interest fees on credit cards. Buy-one-get-ones. Flash sales. Everywhere you look there's a place to spend your hard-earned money and, unfortunately, get yourself further into debt. But if YOU decide that those things can't enter your sphere of spending, then you'll learn how to simply ignore them. Here are a couple of things that really helped us block out the you-must-buy-this-thing-now noise:

- We used unroll.me to unsubscribe our emails from EVERY company we could buy things from (remember, it's not forever!).

- We unfollowed retail accounts on Twitter or Instagram to avoid posts with tempting discounts and deals.

- We stopped giving each other material gifts on Valentine's Day, birthdays, Christmas, our anniversary, and Arbor Day (an obvious gift-giving opportunity), and instead opted to come up with unique experiences together (more on this in the following chapter on Minimalism).

- We told our families that we were going to be way more frugal and would appreciate their understanding of our limited spending (sounds silly, but clueing in the people you love can be very important).

- We made it essential to tackle this plan and battle the Debt Monster TOGETHER.

That last point was one of the most important ones. By teaming up to pay off our debt, and by making sacrifices together, it felt less like we were doing this on our own and more like we were playing a two-player game. (Remember how cute little Diddy Kong would help Donkey Kong on his banana-fueled benders in Donkey Kong 64? It was always more fun when they played together!)

We both agreed that any purchase over $100, be it for business or life, we would talk over together before buying. You may be thinking, "That would cause World War III in my house!" We thought the same thing, too, initially. However, the more we talked about it, the more it became a running joke. And, the more we talked about the things we wanted to buy, the less things we ended up buying. We kept running into this similar conversation:

Me: Hey babe (yeah, we're a "hey babe" couple, get over it), I want to buy these sweet roller blades.

Caroline: Sup, babe? Um . . . how much are they?

Me: They're normally $300, but they're on sale for $120! It's a great deal! I can live out my childhood fantasy of becoming a professional roller blader!

Caroline: Hmmm . . . let me ask you this. Do you actually need them, or are you just channeling a childhood fantasy that you couldn't have and are now trying to have as a thirty-five-year-old man?

Me: Dammit. You're right. I guess I don't need them. I'll just go watch the movie *Airborne* again.

Silly fictitious convo? Absolutely. But you'd be surprised how many of our conversations went just like that when we started actually talking about buying things.

It's years later now, we're completely debt-free, and we *still* have conversations about purchases over $100. Often times we have conversations about purchases of $20 or $50. The more we talk to each other about spending money, the more we're forced to explain the reasoning behind our purchases—to each other and, more important, to ourselves. That's often when we realize we don't actually want what we're thinking about buying, we're just being persuaded by incredibly good marketing.

What if you don't have a significant other to team up with? Let's talk about the buddy system! Here are a few ways to use the power of accountability and find someone to talk finances with:

1. I am willing to bet the shirt off my back you have people closer to you than you think who are dealing with debt. Go to your close friends, your trusted confidants, and talk to them about debt. If they're willing to talk honestly about money and debt, ask them if they're willing to team up and fight off the Debt Monster side by side. Working together with someone who's on the same financial journey as you (or struggle, if we're being honest) can be such a huge game changer when it comes to finally making a change.

2. Can't find a friend? Talk to your family members. It can be weird to navigate financial waters within a family. However, odds are you have someone in your familial circle who has dealt with (or is dealing with) debt. Ask around. It's time to stop hiding behind your debt and feeling ashamed of it. It's time to beat that boss level and finish the game of debt for good!

3. Find a noncrusty financial advisor. Noncrusty financial planners are waiting to help you get out of debt, and you don't need to be rich to hire them. What do I mean by noncrusty? I mean: not old. I don't know why, but I always imagined financial planners as old guys wearing those green poker visors and pulling back the arm on a rusty calculating machine. We were introduced to our financial advisors (we have a team of two) through friends we trust and they have been incredibly helpful for advice and talking through some of our debt payoff strategies. You may be thinking, *But Jason, I don't know any friends who have good financial planners* and to that I'd say: "head to Yelp.com, no joke!" If you're in the USA, it's very easy to find a well-vetted financial advisor in your local area using Yelp. If you're not in the USA, I'd recommend continuing to ask friends and family for recommendations.

4. Be a damn rock star, pull up your pants, and make it happen on your own! Now, I don't recommend this to everyone. But if you're a go-getter and you typically don't need help getting things done, take the steps I've written in this chapter and start applying them immediately. Here's how you know if you are a go-getter and can do this on your own: you actually already started your own expense spreadsheet and were starting to calculate the money you could be saving before reading this sentence.

STOP BEING EMBARRASSED
AND ASHAMED OF YOUR DEBT

I know I mentioned this before, but if you're in debt right now it bears repeating. Debt sucks. It's stressful. It keeps you up at night. I've been there. But it's even worse if you continue to bottle up your feelings about your debt and continue ignoring it.

Money is a game. It's a completely made-up thing in our society that started, not as coins, paper, and plastic cards, but basically as clamshells and the furs of animals. Think about that fact for minute—you're basically ashamed of the fact that you owe someone way too many beaver pelts. Well, as they say, beaver pelts don't grow on trees. You aren't going to just find a bunch of beaver pelts lying around in your office or on the side of the road. You have to drive to the beaver pelt store and get some! Okay . . . you get my drift. Money is made-up.

We have this emotional attachment to money. You've probably felt it, maybe even as recently as this week or month. You paid for something and it felt like you were letting a piece of yourself go. Stop doing this and repeat after me: Money is a game. Money is made-up.

You make money. You spend money. Some people have very little money. Some people have a yacht overflowing with beaver pelts. It's the world we live in, but if there's one thing I want you to take away from this chapter, it's to stop attaching your self-worth and your emotions to how much money you have (or don't have). Stop attaching your self-worth to your net worth.

Right this very minute, you can make more money. You absolutely can. You can put your couch on Craigslist. You can get a part-time job at Starbucks or Target. You can sell the beaver pelts you keep in your attic. Heck, you can set up a lemonade stand at the end of your block. That's how ridiculously easy it is to make money.

Now, are those sustainable money-making options? Not at all. But again, making money is just a game and if you want to get to the next level, you have to decide to change your perspective.

We made the decision that $124,094 was a game in life we wanted to win. Pay off an extra $15,000 in the first year? Bazinga! Level completed! Have an extra

$5,000 from a business venture? Pazow! Next level completed. Get $200 from Grama for my birthday (as a thirty-two-year-old man)? Cha-chinga! Another (smaller) level completed.

Level by level. Dollar by dollar. I started to win the game of debt. And you can do the same thing if you shift your perspective and stop letting the embarrassment and shame of your debt control your actions.

On June 12, 2016, fifteen months after we first made our get-out-of-debt pact, we paid off our final credit card balance in one final sum ($9,639). We beat the boss! We won the debt game! It. Felt. Ahhhhhhhhmazing. Overcoming such a huge financial obstacle is one of the best feelings I've ever had. I know that sounds crazy, but the emotional toll that being in debt can take on you is real. If you're dealing with debt or financial struggles right now, I hope this story serves as motivation for you and shows you it is possible to dig yourself out of that hole.

INTENTIONAL SPLURGING: BALANCING SAVING WITH LIVING

Now, I do want to mention that with all this debt and saving money talk, there is one huge caveat. I do not believe in extreme saving at the expense of living. I *do* believe having some form of savings and covering your ass-ets (hehe, see what I did there?) is a good thing. However, for me and my values, I view this idea of saving for the future in a bit of a weird way (if you can imagine that?).

Saving for "retirement" has always felt ridiculous to me. Why? Mostly because every retired person I know lives a pretty damn boring life—at least by my standards. I don't view my life as being chopped into two sections, my working years and leisure years. I want a long, full life where work and leisure are woven together until the end. This is why the notion of a giant pile of money waiting for me when I'm older just doesn't feel necessary to me. Yes, I want *enough* money saved that I don't have to stress about money or worry about health, but it's incredibly important to me to balance that with enjoying my life NOW.

The conventional mindset when it comes to saving money is that you want to hoard as much of it as you can. You're supposed to stockpile it and watch that sum grow so you get to enjoy it later on. Okay fine, but what about the potential apocalypse? Or what if a meteor hit Earth tomorrow? Or what if, just what if, and I'm sorry this is morbid, what if I was diagnosed with a terminal illness and only had six months to live? My point is, I don't want to sock all my resources away for an uncertain future when all I have is the present.

Life is too short to wait until after retirement to live it.

What this means for me is that yes, we save, but we also make sure we spend. (I know, this may be confusing coming from the guy who just talked about paying off debt and spending less for an entire chapter, but bear with me. Like most things in life, my opinions on money aren't just black and white.)

I believe spending, *with intention* (that's the key), can be as important as saving. Money can't buy happiness, but it can buy experiences—and experiences can shape who you are and how you feel. This is why we try to take one or two big trips per year. This is why I recently spent about $400 on coffee-making supplies. This is why we splurge on a day at the spa or a fancy dinner from time to time. I don't want to enjoy my life when it's nearing the end; I want to enjoy it all the way through.

Even though we are intentional about splurging, we get down to the nitty-gritty to make sure we're not overextending ourselves. (This is how we *stay* out of debt.) Along with a weekly budget meeting, we also have a long meeting before the beginning of each new year where we project out how much we plan to make and how much we plan to spend that year. The way we do our financial projections looks something like this:

- Start a new Google Spreadsheet (or Airtable)

- List the months of the year across the top rows

- List our business projects/income streams in the first column

- Make very conservative guesses on monthly income for each project

- List out our expected monthly expenses (personal and business) by category (eating out, rent, shopping, travel, etc.) with a budget total for each category

- Subtract our monthly expenses from our monthly income to give us our "surplus"

- Subtract and set aside our estimated taxes from our surplus

- Decide how much of our surplus we want to save

- Use the remaining money for intentional splurging and enjoying life

Every month, along with tracking our spending and keeping an eye on our expenses budget, we update these projections with the actuals and adjust accordingly. Yes, I may have *wanted* to rent a fun sports car for that road trip but if we're not on track with our business revenue, we might want to hold off on making that splurge.

Like most things in life, it's all a balancing act. Just like we didn't get out of debt overnight, we didn't start making $100,000/year overnight. Everything involving money takes time, sacrifice, and a willingness to reject the way things have always been done in order to develop saving and spending habits that fit *your* unique values and lifestyle. There's always another answer. There's always something else to try. There's always a weird way you can make some additional money. It's up to you to challenge your existing circumstances (and biases) and work toward the financial situation that will make you the happiest.

Chapter 8: "Own it!" recap and to-do item

- If you're jazzed up about building your own debt payoff plan I encourage you to go to wanderingaimfully.com/debt after reading this section. You'll find an even more in-depth story of how we paid off all our debt but you'll also find our example spreadsheets and tasks for organizing expenses, doing revenue projections, and building a debt payoff plan that is specific to YOUR situation.

CHAPTER 9

Minimalism

One of the most impactful changes I've made in my life has been becoming a minimalist. If that word turns you off, I ask that you let me explain the benefits of minimalism before you run the other direction. And if I haven't lost you after that, I'd also love to share with you why I believe with every fiber of my being that you should try to find your own flavor of minimalism, too.

Before I go on, let's get clear on how I define minimalism. **To me, minimalism is the idea that you can live with less, but get *more* out of life.** It is the idea that you consciously only allow things into your life that you believe will bring you value.

Now, let's briefly go over what minimalism is not. Minimalism is not living in a home with just one chair, and minimalism is not a cult that keeps you from buying things ever again. Minimalism is different for everyone because each person's notion of what brings them value is as unique as their fingerprint.

A few years ago, I was *not* a minimalist. I was an electronic gadget–buying machine. Amazon Prime and I were in a serious, committed relationship. I loved that little retail high I'd get with a new purchase. I thought that buying new things would make me happy, and oh, I bought the heck out of them.

I expertly justified buying new things, especially moderately expensive things. I convinced myself that because I had the financial ability, I should compensate for all the times in my youth when I wanted things but couldn't have them.

All of those thoughts, buying habits, and societal pressures came to a screeching halt in late May 2013 when Caroline and I heard a guy named Joshua Fields Millburn tell his story at an event called Misfit Con. It's not an exaggeration to say that hearing Joshua speak that day changed my life.

The short version is this: Joshua had a job that paid him well, but he was constantly buying things to try to fill a void in his life. When he realized he was unhappy and that all the material stuff in his life was weighing him down, he decided to do something about it. In order to simplify, he followed the advice of his best friend Ryan and decided to explore becoming a minimalist.

His transformation didn't happen overnight. In fact, it was more of a slow transition away from buying lots of things than it was a stark, cold-turkey quitting frenzy. Slowly, Joshua parted ways with his stuff while he worked to change his other habits. The by-product of doing those things? He and his friends started to notice a pretty extreme spike in his happiness. (Together Joshua and Ryan now run a blog with millions of visitors, TheMinimalists.com.)

At the time I heard Joshua speak, I was in crushing debt from trying to keep IWearYourShirt afloat when it was no longer profitable. I was desperate for anything that would help alleviate the pressure of debt and allow me to take back control over my finances again. I was also simply getting older and realizing that expensive cars and an Amazon Prime membership were not the secret to a happy life.

Joshua's story inspired Caroline and me to take a good look at our lives (and our things). We took inventory of all of the stuff throughout our home, and we asked ourselves an important question we learned from Joshua: does this thing bring me value?

CLOSET CLEAROUT

It started with the closet. This was the place in our home where we had accumulated a bunch of items but had rarely let anything go. Shorts I hadn't worn since college? Piled in a drawer. T-shirts Caroline used to wear for her sorority? Stuffed on the back of a shelf. Jeans we both bought on sale because, hey, we thought our butts would look great in them? Never worn and covered in closet dust (our butts will never know how great they would have looked).

Instead of trying to make a bunch of one-by-one decisions as we combed through hangers and drawers, we instead decided to draw a more drastic boundary: If we hadn't worn it in a year, it had to go.

The result? We filled multiple garbage bags to the brim with clothing we hadn't worn in years and had only held onto 'just in case we might want to wear them again someday.' Someday hadn't come in all the years prior, though, so it was high time we got honest with ourselves about whether we actually planned to wear any of those neglected items.

Shortly after that first closet clean-out, Caroline discovered the concept of having a capsule wardrobe. This meant she pared down her wardrobe to just thirty-three items (not including underwear). It turns out that having thirty items she really loved was way more satisfying than an overstuffed closet full of things she only half-heartedly liked.

She also used the closet clearout as an opportunity to make a few extra bucks. At first, she put together an itemized list of all the clothes she wanted to sell. A $30 dress here. A $15 blouse there (yes, I know what a blouse is!). She listed a few items on a resale website called Threadflip, taking photos and typing up descriptions for each item. The longer the list got though, the more Caroline dreaded having to sell these items individually.

I saw the look on her face, so I asked her one of my infamously weird *why* questions: "Why don't you just ask if someone wants to buy all of it for $500?"

She was slow to answer me at first, but she finally shook her head. "No way . . . There's no way anyone would pay $500 for all my already-worn clothing."

Did she have a lapse in memory, forgetting that people used to pay me to wear T-shirts? Maybe! So I encouraged her the best I could in that moment. "I think you'd be surprised. Plus . . . you don't get what you don't ask for!"

Having been together for a few years at that point, Caroline knew that once I pull out the secret weapon (the phrase "you don't get what you don't ask for"), the battle has already been lost. You can't argue with that phrase! (Well, unless you're asking for something utterly ridiculous . . . like, a lifetime subscription to Elon Musk's thoughts. You probably can't get that just by asking, but you see what I mean.)

Caroline wasn't sure how this was going to go down, but she put together a collage of photos anyway because why not? She wrote out all the pieces that would be sold in her $500 bundle of gently preworn clothing, and then she posted it on Instagram with a link to a buy button (using Gumroad.com) where someone could pay for it. I won't make you guess what happened next. In just a few hours, she had $500 from one person, and was done selling her clothing. Just. Like. That. (And that is why we test our assumptions, ladies and gentlemen!)

Cleaning out our wardrobes (on multiple occasions) has helped us enjoy the clothing we do have a lot more. Gone are the days when we used to stand in our packed-to-the-hilt closets, paralyzed by too many choices. Because of this one area where we found our own flavor of minimalism, we have just the right amount of clothes, and we actually like all of them. Adding a new piece of clothing becomes more of a question about "do I *need* this?" rather than "do I *want* this?"

A few things have come out of this more minimal approach to shopping. We save a lot of money (money that we can put toward experiences like travel rather than material things.) We keep our closets lean with only things that we love and wear regularly. Getting dressed in the morning takes zero decision-making power. I even went through a period where I wore just seven T-shirts in rotation, one for each day of the week. You have no idea how freeing it is to enjoy everything in your closet and not have to think twice about what you put on in the morning. Travel packing has become especially easy because I can literally fit almost my entire wardrobe in a travel backpack. No decision-making required. I actually get a weird thrill now from going into a retail store and walking out with nothing.

After our first major closet purge, we kept getting rid of things until our closets were as lean as possible. But the way we keep them that way is through the "1-in-1-out rule." This means that for every new item that comes into our closet, one older item has to be donated, especially if there's a similar item already in our wardrobe. Buy a new pair of jeans? An existing pair has to go. Buy a new awesome scarf? Sorry, old crappy scarf, you have to leave. Buy three pairs of zany socks from Happy Socks? Three pairs of old boring socks are out the door. Buh-bye.

This rule forces us to be thoughtful about every clothing purchase. We have to be picky about what we want to buy because, if we make a purchase, we have to be willing to let something else go. It also insures that we're not just adding to the number of things we own, but we're constantly cultivating and curating the thoughtful things we choose to hold on to.

MINIMIZING BUSINESS BAGGAGE

Aside from our closets, in the early days of adopting a more minimal lifestyle, we became aware of just how much stuff we were stashing away at our house and holding onto for emotional reasons. The biggest contributor to this had to be my leftover IWearYourShirt memorabilia.

You'd be amazed how much stuff a T-shirt wearing operation would leave behind. After the business closed, I was left with boxes of silly props, filming equipment, random papers, and a T-shirt–themed wall mural—all the things that helped me create daily photo and video content for that business while it was active.

Long after I closed the business, all of these items still took up space in my home. They stared me in the face and were constant reminders of a business that was no more. The memories these items were connected to were both good and bad, but the longer this stuff stayed in my home, the more stuck in the past I felt.

When I finally got rid of all the leftover stuff from IWearYourShirt, an incredible thing happened. A weight lifted off my shoulders—a weight that I didn't even know was as heavy as it was. With letting the physical baggage go, I could let go of the mental baggage, too. Imagine that.

Do you have an old business or job or idea from which you have kept related items? Do you have a stage of your life you're still holding onto emotionally by keeping stuff because it makes you feel good? Maybe it's time to let those things go. It's important to remember that the memories don't live inside the things; they live inside you. Start small, and see if you feel lighter once you let go. My guess is that you, too, will experience that sense of relief and you'll only begin to crave more of that streamlined, white space—both physically and emotionally.

GIFTS AND HOLIDAYS

Our closets and items around the house were just the beginning of incorporating minimalism into our lives. Once we started to feel the freedom and space of letting things go, it started to affect every purchasing decision we made—including gifts. We decided together that we no longer wanted to buy each other gifts for birthdays or holidays. Instead, we decided we'd celebrate these things by creating memorable experiences.

This changes from year to year for our birthdays, but for Christmas it's fun because it encourages us to come up with creative traditions to look forward to. For example, on Christmas each of us surprises the other by picking a movie, a snack, and an activity for us both to enjoy. (Mine: *Arthur Christmas*, hot chocolate, origami. Hers: *Home Alone*, chocolate-covered popcorn, building gingerbread houses.) Not only do we fill an entire evening with laughter and fun, we've created a new tradition we'll carry forward and remember for years. Truthfully, that's more than we can say for anything we've given each other over the years that was wrapped in a box and put under the tree.

Holidays, and the subsequent gift-giving they bring, can be especially challenging. While we've figured this out for ourselves, we haven't quite figured it out with our families. It's hard to fight traditions that have been around for years, and it's hard to tow the line between doing things differently in your own life vs. forcing your beliefs on other people. I bring this up not because I have a solution (yet), but because it's important to share that choosing minimalism doesn't mean you can just shut down your other loved ones' ways of expressing affection. It's about sharing your perspective and your reasons behind your decisions with your family. You can express to them why material things are less important to you than experiences and quality time, and they may come around to a more minimal approach to the holidays. Your family may find your decision to have less stuff weird, but that's okay because this book is all about owning YOUR weird, not changing the opinions of the people around you.

FINDING YOUR OWN
FLAVOR OF MINIMALISM

Obviously, your version of minimalism is going to look completely different from mine, but that's the point of this chapter and the entire message of the Own Your Weird approach to life. The decisions you make, the things you value, and how you live with less clutter—both physical and mental—are the nuances that will make your flavor of minimalism unique.

It all goes back to those values we talked about in Section I. Once you identify what's important to you, you can begin making more conscious and considered choices when it comes to what you buy.

If you're stuck with how to explore becoming a minimalist, the best thing to do is just start trying different things. See what sticks for you. See what makes you happier. Give the idea of having less a chance and try to measure how it makes you feel.

Chapter 9: "Own it!" recap and to-do item

- It's a minimalist challenge ladies and gentlemen! This weekend, I challenge you to do your own closet clearout. Grab your significant other, a few garbage bags, throw on your favorite Spotify playlist, and anything in your closet you haven't worn in a year gets donated. Don't have a significant other? Have a friend join you and then move to their closet after your closet is done. Trust me on this one, you'll feel a weight lifted off your shoulders (and it's not just because you're donating that jacket with the atrociously large shoulder pads in it!).

CHAPTER 10

Choosing Adventure

When Caroline and I started dating, I remember driving to my favorite sub sandwich shop and her posing the question, "Could you ever see yourself living somewhere else?"

First of all, we'd only been dating for a few weeks. Pump. The. Brakes. (Actually, I think I did pump the physical brakes in the car due to the hard-hitting question.)

I answered, "I don't think so. I've lived in multiple other states and cities, and I really like Florida. I could see myself living here forever."

Long pause.

"Yeah, me too," she finally said (after I had a mini heart attack wondering if our relationship was over before it even started). And that was the last time we ever brought up the subject of living anywhere else for years.

The truth is, I liked the life we had built in our little area of Ponte Vedra Beach, just outside Jacksonville, Florida. We both had our families nearby. The ocean was a five-minute drive away. I owned a house in a quiet subdivision. There was a lot to like.

Throughout the years I was building IWearYourShirt, I traveled a ton. I flew around the country doing speaking engagements, so I got my taste of different cities with different vibes. Yet I always loved coming home to Florida. Or was it something else I loved coming home to? Looking back, I can see that what I actually loved about it wasn't the location itself; it was the comfort of my routines.

I was constantly pushing and working and "hustling" at this big weird risk I had taken professionally (IWearYourShirt), so having my low-key suburban beach life was comforting. It was simple and predictable.

However, once things with IWearYourShirt started taking a downturn in 2012, I began looking around for other local entrepreneurs to turn to—people who could understand what I was going through. That's when I started to realize all the friends I was turning to for support didn't live near me. The idea started to creep in that maybe there was a community of more like-minded people elsewhere.

Once 2014 rolled around, I had written my first book and purged so many different emotions and stories from the IWearYourShirt era. It was a time of major transition, and I was looking for a fresh start. A new personal challenge. That's the first time Caroline and I brought up the idea of moving away from Jacksonville, a place I'd been for over ten years and where Caroline was born and raised. By that time, we were different people than those versions of ourselves that wanted to stay put in Florida forever. Our values had changed, and so our outlook on moving was changing, too. We were ready for a weird change, and I think you're going to find this ranks right up there on the weird scale!

With this new itch to explore fresh in our minds, Caroline and I attended our favorite event of the year, Misfit Con in Fargo, ND (a different year, but the same event where we initially saw Joshua Fields Millburn and embraced minimalism). This was our third year attending the incredibly special and bespoke event put on by our friends AJ and Melissa Leon. AJ and Melissa chose to hold the event in Fargo each year partially because it's an incredibly cool and welcoming town, perfect for artists and creators, but also partially to introduce the city to people from all over who may not have ever thought to travel there. I remember walking the streets of the quaint downtown, an amazing cup of hand-crafted coffee in my hand, thinking to myself: "I wonder how many other cities out there exist like this just waiting to be discovered." This itch was becoming more than just a passing thought; it was becoming something we both couldn't get out of our minds.

TAKING THE LEAP

There we were at Misfit Con Year 3, and we decided to go out to a nice lunch with friends in between speakers during the conference. At lunch, the conversation casually turned to moving. Two of our friends, Clay Hebert and Julia Roy, lived in Manhattan, but they were growing tired of the craziness of the city and were itching for a change, too. Since they both worked for themselves like us, a big move was really just a matter of deciding.

Some of the cities Caroline and I had discussed hypothetically at that point were Portland, Austin, San Diego—places that weren't huge cities but still had great food and an entrepreneurial scene.

"Where are you guys thinking of moving?" I asked Clay and Julia.

"We're not sure, maybe Portland, Austin, or San Diego," Clay replied.

Wait. What? I remember thinking. *Is Clay a mind-reader? Is he navigating my brain-space and sharing my own thoughts back to me?*

I responded, "Uhhh, those are the exact cities we're thinking about moving to as well."

(At this point, I should probably come clean and tell you there *was* alcohol involved at this meal. Nothing like a few tequila-infused afternoon cocktails to get the weird idea wheels to start spinning.)

Julia half-jokingly chimed in, "We should just all move in together and have an awesome entrepreneur pad!"

"If we lived together, we could get a really cool place, probably something none of us could afford on our own! So . . . which city?" I asked.

"I lived in San Diego a few years ago and loved it. You can't beat the weather. Plus, there are a bunch of other entrepreneurs I know out there," Clay added.

"That's it. We're moving to San Diego and living together. LET'S DO THIS!" I yelled, while cheering with whatever drink I currently had in my hand.

Now . . . you may have found yourself in a conversation like this among friends (and cocktails) sometime where things end in some wild resolution to do XYZ. "Let's start a business! Cheers!" or . . . "Let's buy a vineyard! Cheers!" or . . . "Let's all fly to the Maldives! Cheers!" The dangerous thing about making these kinds of plans at a table with me, though? My brain immediately goes to *how-can-we-make-this-happen* mode. As I told you, this idea had been percolating for a while, so when confronted with an opportunity to not just talk about *maybe* moving, but to actually do it, I was ready to take the leap.

(You may notice something about the retelling of that conversation . . . Where was Caroline in all of this? Well, she was at the table. But I think my typical whirlwind of energy and excitement when an idea hits me had blindsided her into silence. Either that or the brunch was especially delicious. I had margaritas, so I wasn't really paying attention. We did eventually have a level-headed discussion about what it would take to move, and just like me, she couldn't really come up with a good reason to stay in Florida. We both knew it was time for a new chapter.)

Just like that, we made the decision to move to San Diego. Not only that, but we decided to move to San Diego and actually cohabitate with another couple. (There's definitely some magic in the air of Fargo, North Dakota. If you're worried you might uproot your life, you may not want to visit or attend a Misfit Con.) In the following few months, we started keeping our eyes out for rental properties in San Diego. We had Skype calls with Clay and Julia to figure out if living together was actually a good idea. With every tiny step we took, it started to become more and more real. We even flew out to San Diego twice to stay in an Airbnb with Clay and Julia and go neighborhood/house hunting, until we finally found the absolute perfect sprawling house in a suburb north of San Diego called Poway.

THE "EVERYTHING MUST GO!" SALE

I know I'm making this whole "move across the country" thing sound so easy, but trust me, after we made the leap, the very real logistical challenge of moving finally set in. Once we signed the rental agreement on our new place in San Diego, the only remaining question was what to do with everything we had in our sixteen-hundred-square-foot home in Florida.

As you now know, thanks to our shift to minimalism, we'd already gone through old boxes of stuff and downsized considerably. If you visited our home in 2014, you probably would have thought we had very little stuff. But for anyone who has ever moved, you know that stuff hides in all the crevices, cracks, closets, attics, and any places storable items can find a home for themselves.

Once we'd found a place in San Diego, signed the rental agreement, and picked the date to move, the clock was ticking. As someone with plenty of experience selling things on eBay and Craigslist, I knew we could get rid of some of our stuff fairly quickly. But that begged the question: should we pay for a rental truck to move the last of our stuff clear across the country, or should we just get rid of everything and start fresh with only what we could squeeze into our Volkswagen Tiguan? The latter feels a bit *own your weird*, no?

This was a conversation Caroline and I had multiple times. So we took to a spreadsheet to compare the costs (as you well know by now, we're a spreadsheet kind of family!).

Here's what the calculations looked like:

- **Option A: Pack it up and move**—A house-sized moving truck would cost around $3,000 for a cross-country rental truck to put our last remaining possessions in.

- **Option B: Sell everything and start fresh**—Selling EVERYTHING left in our home would give us a profit of around $4,500, and then realistically, we figured buying all new furniture and home stuff would cost us about $10,000–$12,000 (for a net cost of about $7,500).

This is the part where I tell you we chose Option A because it was cheaper and we were still trying to save money, right? Well, that's what I initially thought. But the more I thought about driving a big, unwieldy rental truck nearly 2,372 miles, the more it stressed me out. What happens if we get a flat tire somewhere in the middle of Texas? What happens if the rental truck gets hit by something and ruins our stuff inside? How will I keep my sanity driving a vehicle that has the interior accommodations of a 1981 Ford Taurus?

Financially speaking, selling all of our stuff wasn't the better choice, but it was the one that gave us the best peace of mind and a fresh start. So that's what we did. (These are decisions that become a lot clearer once you learn how to spend your money through the lens of your values, by the way.)

But how did we sell all of our stuff and not have it drive us (mostly me, the logistics manager) insane? I certainly didn't want to list every item in our home. So, we busted a "Buy Caroline's Whole Wardrobe on Instagram for $500" move and decided instead to have an "Everything Must Go!" sale out of our house, just like a big furniture store closeout sale. (Oversight on our part that we didn't get some of those neon store window signs. It really would have completed the look.) We planned to do it on a Saturday, just a few days before we would pack up our small Volkswagen SUV, and make the journey across the country with only what we could fit inside the vehicle.

We had announced our sale on social media accounts (one of the few times Facebook did in fact come in handy) to give people a few days' notice. I also took a few hours to text message everyone in my phone that lived in Jacksonville to tell them about the impending house-emptying sale.

That Saturday morning, I woke up a few hours before our sale officially started, which we set for 10 a.m. After a few hours of organizing and photographing, we were ready to "open the doors" and let our rabid buyers in. (In all seriousness, there were actually people parked outside the house as early as 8:30 waiting for us to kick off the sale. People are serious about getting a good deal!).

It's a funny thing to have hoards of strangers come into your home, haggling with you on the price of your once-coveted items. A very specific lamp you remember searching the depths of the Internet for, being sold for one-quarter of the price? It seems like it would be disheartening. But, in truth, it felt oddly liberating. We kept reminding ourselves: it's only stuff! Thing after thing. Item after item. Our little home was getting emptier and emptier, and we were feeling lighter and lighter. But, that's not to say everything was easy to part with.

So many things in our home had stories and memories attached to them. But what you realize when you start parting with those things is: the memories don't go with them. As I said before, the memories don't live in the things—they live in our minds. Experiencing that lesson on a house-sized scale definitely helped me detach myself from physical possessions on a new level.

Now you may be wondering, did people bring hundreds of dollars in cash? Or write you checks? And the answer is . . . Nope! Thanks to the handy-dandy Square credit card reader, I operated our Everything Must Go sale like a small brick-and-mortar business owner. Swiping credit cards left and right, sending people email receipts like a boss.

When the day ended, we had successfully gotten rid of 95 percent of the things in our home. There were a handful of larger items that were purchased but were still sitting in our garage waiting for buyers to come by with a truck or large vehicle to haul them off. (Part of the plan for doing the sale on a Saturday was to use the following Sunday to offload any remaining items.)

In total, we made $5,200 from our Everything Must Go! sale (better than my initial projection!). We were able to completely empty out our entire home in one weekend and we were officially ready for our move.

CHOOSING ADVENTURE
∙∙∙∙∙∙∙∙∙∙∙∙∙∙∙∙∙∙∙∙∙∙∙∙∙∙∙∙∙∙∙∙∙∙∙∙∙∙∙

The drive west from Florida to California was, thankfully, pretty uneventful. We took the less scenic route to get to our new digs as soon as possible, making four stops at various LaQuinta Inns along the way (shout out to LaQuinta Hotels for being pet friendly!) Our SUV was packed to the brim with all the remaining things we owned, though we still left two seats' worth of space in the back for our dog Plaxico. He's pretty particular about needing to travel in comfort. In between the music, podcasts, and audiobooks, Caroline and I talked about the excitement and uncertainty of making such a huge move like this.

Many people go their entire lives staying in one place. Staying in one job. Never experiencing different and unique things. It may be the fear of the unknown, or the limitations people put on themselves, but for whatever reason, there are so many people who never take that leap to see what's possible on the other side. Caroline and I had done adventurous things in our businesses, but this was truly a big adventurous thing we were choosing to do in our lives. It added difficulty. It completely obliterated our existing (and comfortable) routines. But, as our good friend and co-creator of Misfit Con, AJ Leon, likes to say: "This is not your practice life." We knew if we didn't follow that spark of curiosity, we'd likely regret it.

Once we got settled in our new home with our roommates Clay and Julia, we began to create our new lives. We developed new routines. We established new schedules for ourselves. We got adjusted to the time zone difference (which is still a bit weird, even years later.)

For that first year, we met lots of new friends who, upon hearing about our big move from Florida, almost always asked some version of this question: *What made you move out here to the West Coast?*

We would answer simply and succinctly with a grin on our faces every time: **Adventure.**

The surprise on their faces was always so satisfying. They were waiting for us to say something like "for a job" or another opportunity—some catalyst or reason that had brought us to this city on the other side of the country. You could see their eyes light up when they realized the only catalyst was us. We *decided* to pursue something weird and different for our lives, and so we did. We chose adventure.

There's a very powerful feeling that comes with choosing adventure in your life and business. It puts you in control. It shows you that you are the master of your own domain and decisions. But, choosing adventure, much like doing anything differently, isn't always easy.

It would have been easier for us to stay in our perfectly comfortable lives in Florida. We wouldn't have had to clear out our home. We could have saved money. We could have avoided some difficult conversations that went along with leaving our families and friends.

Even still, if we ultimately did decide to move to California, it probably would have been easier to find a place on our own. Living with roommates, especially as adults, brings its own unique challenges. But, learning to navigate our new adventure *was* the adventure itself.

It may be easier for you to avoid taking any kind of leap in your life right now. In fact, I know it is. Routines and comfort zones are exactly that: easy. They're what you're used to. They come second nature to you. But growth doesn't come from staying in your comfort zones.

Comfort zones are like quicksand—slowly pulling you into their depths and making it harder and harder for you to eventually fight your way out.

Adventure doesn't have to mean skydiving or spelunking or backpacking around the world. It could mean making a decision to go in a different direction with where you live or who you are currently in a relationship with.

It may be especially tempting for you to avoid adventure in your business right now. There's no doubt that following the tactics, strategies, and blueprints created by other people feels easier. But, as you now know, owning your weird isn't about doing things that work for other people. It's about doing what's right for you.

To truly get to that coveted "next level," you have to be willing to take risks. You have to be willing to seek out the adventurous options.

Choosing adventure in your life or business comes down to deciding how much you're willing to sacrifice to find out what's on the other side of adventure. For the most part, you know what's on the other side of your current circumstances. You see those every day. But if you're willing to sacrifice what's comfortable (and destroy your comfort zones), you may find some incredibly rewarding experiences waiting for you.

Chapter 10: "Own it!" recap and to-do item

- What adventure are you ready to choose for your life? It doesn't have to be moving clear across the country and selling all of your stuff, but is there some idea that's been twinkling in the back of your mind? Is there some decision where choosing *adventure* may feel uncomfortable but can help you live the Own Your Weird mindset? It's time to choose adventure, and when you do, send me an email or a tag me in a post about it on social media (reminder: I'm @jasondoesstuff)!

CHAPTER 11

Food and Health

When you decided to purchase this book, I imagine you didn't think to yourself, "I can't wait to hear what Jason has to say about paleo diets, veganism, and random other food and health things!" But alas dear reader, you are about to hop aboard the food and health monorail. Hold on tight to the nearest grab handle, and please stand clear of the metaphorical doors.

You may be wondering how food relates to owning your weird. Well, funny enough, if there's one aspect of my life that has been impacted the most by questioning convention and navigating my own winding path to arrive at a place that's uniquely right for me, it's actually my health. Over the past five years especially, I've made pretty big shifts in what I eat and how I view health in general, all with the intention of creating a lifestyle blueprint that's completely on my own weird terms.

Much like the beliefs we form about business or life "rules," the ideas about what we should eat and what's considered "healthy" are very much informed by the messages we get from the media.

To illustrate my point I want you to be honest about the FIRST thought that comes to your mind when I say the word "milk."

Did you immediately think "does a body good?" Or that milk is a great source of calcium (or, a more recent marketing message, protein?). Or maybe you conjured up an image of a milk mustache (which is incredibly gross if you really think about what milk actually is . . . you know, liquid fat and protein from the udder of a female bovine. Do we really think it's cute to see that stained above another human's mouth?). I'm just saying . . . it's amazing what you start to see when you really *think* about these messages we're all spoon-fed (pun intended—heyo!). But have you ever actually looked up the scientific facts about milk? The actual, real proven data, about what milk is and if it, in reality, "does the body good?"

Okay, indulge me for just a moment. Let me hit you with two science-backed facts[2] about milk: (1) A recent analysis of twelve cohort studies (which included more than five hundred thousand women) found that women with high intakes of lactose—equivalent to that of three cups of milk per day—had a higher risk of ovarian cancer compared to women with the lowest lactose intakes. (2) And in a Harvard study of male health professionals, men who drank two or more glasses of milk a day were almost twice as likely to develop advanced prostate cancer as those who didn't drink milk at all.

So, does milk *really* do a body good? Or are we as a society taking what we hear through the media outlets as gospel? Let's go out on a limb when it comes to these facts and say they're only 1 percent true: isn't the smarter decision to avoid something like milk and get our essential nutrients from other sources if it's super easy and affordable? (Spoiler alert: it is.)

Listen, I know I'm soapboxing a bit here, and I don't mean to pick on milk specifically, but the only reason I'm doing so is to demonstrate why I've found myself making big shifts to my diet and health over the past few years. No longer do I simply trust what I think I know about food, health, and wellness without questioning where my information originally came from.

Up until my early thirties, I was a meat-eating, dairy-loving, protein-promoting guy and no one could tell me anything otherwise. Then I started to ask *why*. I was already questioning other aspects of life and business, shouldn't I question where my food knowledge comes from, too? That's when I decided to start my own experimentation through food and fitness using the Own Your Weird framework to see what worked best for my body and my lifestyle.

FOOD EXPERIMENTS

I have tried virtually every "diet" under the sun. (For the record, when I use the word diet I don't mean some lose-seventeen-pounds-in-seventeen-days soup diet. I'm using the word to reference the selection of foods I eat.) Paleo, gluten-free, bulletproof (yeah, with the butter in the coffee), no processed foods, four-hour body, vegan, raw vegan, and plenty more. Usually these experiments (often thirty days at a time) were brought on by a documentary Caroline and I found on Netflix or by listening to a podcast episode from someone we trust.

I can see now that each of these food experiments followed the Own Your Weird framework pretty closely. First, we'd open ourselves up to the idea that there is no one-size-fits-all diet (goodbye, blueprint). We'd ask ourselves what role we want food to play in our lives and what each of our unique perspectives on food was. We'd identify our values when it comes to determining the right diet for us (things like sustainability, enjoyment, flexibility, etc.). We'd accept any rejection or ridicule that might come from trying out a weird diet and come to grips with whatever sacrifices we needed to make or obstacles we needed to overcome in order to try out something new. Finally, we'd test our assumptions by actually committing to our thirty-day diet experiment. Maybe we assumed going meat-free would be hard or that we'd be hungry all the time, but was that the truth? There was only one way to find out—get out there and test those assumptions.

The biggest lesson I learned from running these different food experiments was just how important it is to pay attention to how food makes me feel. What a weird concept, right? The typical American diet (especially if you eat out a lot) is not necessarily geared toward the foods that are the easiest to digest or the most nutritious. Through experimentation I was able to actually feel the difference in my body from cutting out soda or eating less processed food or avoiding dairy. Approaching changes in our diet with curiosity made me realize just how much time I had spent feeling bad, without realizing those stomachaches, afternoon energy crashes, food comas, or other problems were completely avoidable and related to what I was eating.

THINKING OUTSIDE THE (LUNCH)BOX

Now, I know what you might be thinking by this point. You might be saying to yourself, *I don't have time to switch up my diet.* Or, *I could never eat such-and-such way.* Or *I couldn't do life without my [insert favorite comfort food here.] It's too expensive, too inconvenient, too time-consuming.* And to that I say . . . don't be afraid to think outside the (lunch)box! I look at these things like I look at most things in life: just a set of creative problems that need creative solutions. Even if those solutions are a bit weird by other people's standards.

At the time we started experimenting with shifting our diet, Caroline and I were very much NOT into cooking. We were both working a lot (me trying to get my business going after IWearYourShirt closed down, her trying to start her own creative business) so we, too, had our doubts about food prep and grocery shopping and cutting down on eating out. Until I asked myself: how can we own our weird and think about our daily food intake in a unique way? Can we eat a more conscious, considered diet—without spending loads of time and energy on flipping our eating habits upside down?

After a little research, I came across the idea of using a meal-prep company. I'm not talking about Blue Apron, or any of the companies that mail a box of ingredients to your door. I'm talking about a local company that fully preps and cooks your meals and delivers them to your door, ready to eat with almost zero effort. Umm . . . sign us up, please?

You've probably never looked for a meal-prep company in your area, but all you have to do is hop on Yelp and search for "meal prep." You'll be surprised at how many options there are. If you live in a small town, you may want to search neighboring larger towns or search for "private chef" and reach out to those folks to see if they offer meal prep (many do!).

But, what would it cost? Someone buying and cooking all your food for you—doesn't that get expensive? Well that's the crazy part. Since we were so bad at planning our meals and never wanted to put in the effort to cook, we were actually eating out a lot (with less than healthy options, at that). By using a meal prep company, we actually found that we could save $800 per month from eating out less and not wasting groceries (that's nearly $10,000 per year!). Plus, we estimated we were able to regain forty hours per month by not cooking or shopping for groceries, meaning that time could be spent on our businesses (and bringing more money in the door). So, financially it was actually a great move. Look at that, the Own Your Weird mindset being a positive influence on our financial situation again!

There's not a doubt in my mind that hiring a meal-prep company was the best decision we ever made when it comes to our nutrition. Not only because of the money savings. Not only because of the time savings. But because it took one important step out of the process of trying to eat healthier or shift our diet: using our willpower. When you spend money to have meals prepared for you and you have to use almost no decision-making power to decide what to eat, you always end up making the right choice. Sure, our fridge stocked with prepared meal containers may have looked like we were on an astronaut's diet (it freaked people out when they came over to hang out), but every meal became a no-brainer and helped push us toward the place where we are now, which is a healthy, sustainable, plant-based diet, where we've never felt better or had more energy throughout each day.

EMBRACING A PLANT-BASED DIET

The result of using a meal prep company as a solution to our shifting diet is that we were able to slowly and sustainably shift to the diet that feels like the right thing for our bodies (at this point in our lives): a whole foods, plant-based, mostly grain-free diet. The word that will explain that more easily is vegan. Zero meat. Zero dairy (unless it's unavoidable, like when we took a trip to Italy and found ourselves with virtually no other options, especially if all meat was a no-go). Mostly grain-free. Basically, we just eat a crap-load of vegetables, beans, lentils, nuts, seeds, some fruits, minimal grains, and very little processed food.

You may be making the scream emoji face right now, thinking all of that sounds incredibly restrictive, maybe even weird, and we never enjoy food. But it's actually the opposite! We're both huge foodies and love the joy that comes with a great meal. The difference now is our bodies don't have to pay for it by feeling awful afterward. There are still plenty of amazing flavors and incredibly satisfying foods we love eating.

The key was that we made slow, deliberate changes over time. We stopped looking for the silver bullet (those ever-evasive overnight fixes). Instead, we started replacing the foods we previously loved with healthier alternatives. (For example:

instead of break-and-bake Nestle Tollhouse chocolate chip cookies, I've created my own recipe that's grain-free, sugar-free, guilt-free, and pretty damn tasty!) Making our transition slowly is what allowed us to keep it sustainable. And most important? We've listened to our bodies and found what makes us FEEL the best.

As I mentioned, our transition from a more standard diet (meat, dairy, grains, and some veggies) to a plant-based whole-food diet (veggies, nuts, some grains) didn't happen overnight. It was only after years of reading articles, watching documentaries, talking to vegan friends, listening to podcasts, and going through our own food experiments.

There was, however, one watershed moment for me, and that was reading the book *Eating Animals* by Jonathan Safran Foer. I don't remember the exact reason I decided to read Foer's book, but from the first few pages I knew my days of eating meat were over. I enjoyed the fact that he never set out to write a book that would convert people to a plant-based diet. He simply started to test all his own assumptions about the "standard" American diet, why his family had the food traditions they had (like Thanksgiving turkey), and where all of those decisions were coming from. By the end of writing his book, and through some pretty shocking in-person experiences of the livestock industry, he had convinced himself (and me!) that a plant-based diet was the way to go. If you were to ask me for a first step to see if switching to a plant-based diet is right for you, I'd start with reading *Eating Animals*.

CONSUMERISM AS ACTIVISM

One other amazing benefit to our plant-based diet is that we've stumbled upon the idea of using consumerism as a form of activism. What I mean by that is that we've chosen to eat foods that make us feel the best, but that also have the least impact on the world we live in. Whether you want to stick your head in the sand or not (you silly ostrich), livestock farming is one of the largest contributors to global pollution and carbon emissions. Long-line fishing destroys entire ocean ecosystems. By not supporting the factory-farmed meat or fish industries, in our view we are limiting our impact with our dollars while also investing in the only vessel we get in this crazy thing called life (our amazing human bodies!).

Listen, I have no intention of convincing anyone that our views are "right"— it's not about that. It's just about making sure that if you want the world to be better in a certain way, you have to ask yourself if you're contributing to that better world through the decisions you make (and the dollars you spend). One of the greatest impacts we can make on the world is through what we buy because money, economics, and capitalism largely determine who has decision-making power at scale.

WRAPPING FOOD UP
(GET IT?? ANOTHER FOOD PUN!)

As far as I can tell, we normal people only get one body (I can't speak for people like Tom Cruise, I'm guessing that guy has multiple bodies he can put on whenever he wants). If we aren't making decisions every day, even teeny-tiny ones, that are investments in the long-term well-being of this fleshy vessel we walk around in, was it worth all the tiny fleeting moments of satisfaction from decisions we knew were polluting our bodies? If you know you can make decisions today that give you a healthy and happy life for decades to come, isn't that the only answer?

Don't just accept what you see in commercials or hear in the headlines. Apply the Own Your Weird mindset and start testing all your own assumptions about food (and fitness). Do your own research and draw your own conclusions about what's best for your body. Be okay with the fact that you may eat a "weird" diet by other people's standards.

If there's a final feather to pin in this cap (why we're still putting feathers in caps, I have no idea), it's that your goals regarding food and health should be based on what actually matters to YOU. Not about what you read in magazines. Not about some crazy new four-minute workout app. Not another fad diet that isn't backed by science. Not what your friends and family eat. Focus on what gets you moving, what makes you feel the absolute best, and what is most sustainable for you for the long haul.

Chapter 11: "Own it!" recap and to-do item

- The plant-based eater in me wants you to try eating a plant-based diet for a week and then yell "I OWNED IT!" with all the extra energy and vigor you'll have. But alas, I realize that may be too big of an ask. So, here's what I'd like you to own: Is there ONE thing you can remove from your diet that you know is just plain awful for you (soda, fast food, etc.?). Quit consuming that thing for at least one week. See how you feel afterward. My assumption is you'll thank me and you'll feel better.

CHAPTER 12

Marriage

When Caroline and I first met in 2010, we stayed up way past our respective bedtimes (like, 3 to 4 a.m.) on long phone calls talking and getting to know each other. I come from a family that has had its fair share of divorces, and Caroline's family has had the same thing. Long conversations talking about these shared experiences of navigating blended families and divorces bonded us early on. It was a relief to meet someone who could really relate.

As our relationship went on and we got more serious about each other, the inevitable talks about marriage came up for us. But that's when I realized despite our similarities in background, each of us had a very different idea about what marriage meant and what it could look like for us. Where my family history led me to a general cynicism about the traditional institution of marriage, Caroline's experiences made her even more determined to get married and make it last. We were at a bit of an impasse. It's not an exaggeration to say that many of these conversations ended in frustrated silence, or, even worse, tears (hers . . . mostly), because we both knew we wanted a lifelong commitment but couldn't agree on how that commitment needed to be demonstrated in our lives. Foreshadowing alert: we decided to own our weird with our marriage.

DISCOVERING WHAT MARRIAGE MEANS TO ME

WHY PEOPLE GET MARRIED

One of my sticking points with marriage (besides the grossly obvious divorce-rate statistic) was that people often rush into it, and unfortunately, it seems to be rushed for many reasons that aren't of the couple's own volition. As I saw it, people often decided to tie the knot because of:

- Family pressure: maybe their parents got married young so they feel pressure to follow suit or the parents expect them to "settle down" because it's what their generation all did.

- Friend pressure: all of their friends are getting married, and they don't want to stray too far from the herd or feel like the odd man/woman out.

- Societal pressure: marriage is a behemoth of an industry. Movies, ads, TV shows—they all portray a wedding as the pinnacle of celebration and the "success" of a relationship.

Those are just three types of pressures that people feel when in a relationship, and the problem with all of them is that none of them ask the relationship participants if they feel ready—or even want—to get married.

When Caroline and I started dating, I had just ended a four-year relationship, and she had just ended a one-year relationship. These were both people we'd devoted a sizable amount of time to in our lives, but those relationships didn't work out. I, being on the end of a much longer relationship, knew that even a few years in was only just scratching the surface of truly understanding the person you're with. You don't know how you're going to respond to big life changes or even big changes in each other until you walk through years of challenges together and learn how to come out stronger on the other side.

I understand that for some people, getting married means taking a leap of faith that they'll have to sail uncharted waters together. But for me, I knew I wanted more than faith; I wanted *experience* to prove Caroline and I were well matched to navigate those waters together.

A MARRIAGE VS. A WEDDING

Now I understand that part of our difficulty in coming to an understanding about marriage was that we were both focusing on marriage through the lens of a *wedding*. All I could think of was white gowns, doves, flower petals, and cakes. Ew. It all made me super uncomfortable. It didn't feel like ME at all.

Maybe it was because I hate anything to do with tradition, or maybe it was all the tangled-up emotions I had about weddings and marriage from my family background, but either way, I was fixated on society's projection of The Big White Wedding. As a result, every time Caroline brought up marriage, all I could think was WEDDING, and my immediate next thought: *OHMYGODWHATIHAVEGOTTENMYSELFINTOIWANTTORUNAWAY*." Eventually we stopped having conversations about it because I think Caroline could sense just how much of a hot-button issue it was for me.

Then, one day while sitting in our home office about seven feet from each other, Caroline said something to the effect of: "I just finished reading this article on weddings and I think it helps me understand where you are coming from in your resistance to marriage. Would you please read it?"

"Sure," I said. Because obviously I was (and am) VERY GOOD at noticing vulnerable, emotional moments and responding in a nurturing and healthy way that supports my life partner. Obviously.

Essentially, the article pointed out how our culture pressures us into doing things in a certain socially accepted way, especially as it relates to a wedding. (A core point that clearly resonated with me.) The extravagant reception you'll never forget. The gift registry you have to create with all the things you so desperately need BECAUSE YOU'RE MARRIED NOW AND MARRIED PEOPLE HAVE THINGS.

The article pointed out the stark difference between pouring your energy into a wedding and pouring your energy into a marriage—two very different things. One of the throwaway lines that actually stood out to Caroline was the author posing this question: What if you could only have a wedding AFTER you'd been together for ten years of marriage? Would that make us as a society focus more on finding the right mate and not just wanting the celebration to prove that we fit in with the rest of adult society?

After I finished reading the article (because, emotionally supportive Jason is emotionally supportive), Caroline and I discussed this main point about the difference between a wedding and a marriage. She was finally able to interpret one of my main concerns about getting married, and especially about getting married within the first few years of being in a relationship. Marriage and weddings, as our culture interprets them, didn't seem to really be about making a lifelong commitment to each other; it felt like a show. You don't actually know someone, until you know someone. Knowing that Caroline acknowledged this concern of mine also helped put my mind at ease that she wasn't interested in fulfilling some childhood fantasy of being a bride, but instead wanted what I wanted, which was a partnership that would last.

So, we gave marriage the old Own Your Weird treatment and asked ourselves, if we paid no attention to what society expects us to do, what would marriage look like for us? We talked about a lot of options—never getting married at all, eloping, making up some weird ceremony that only we knew about—but ultimately we loved the idea of using a wedding to celebrate ten years of being together (rather than using it as a "promise" to friends and family that we'd be together forever). No pomp and circumstance; just friends, family, and food to celebrate our love. Then we tabled the conversation for a while, feeling confident that we were finally on the same page.

GETTING MARRIED OUR OWN WEIRD WAY (AKA "HAVING A MARRY-MENT")

AN ÜBER-ROMANTIC PROPOSAL

Fast forward a few years, and we were still both very much on the same page about our ten-year celebratory wedding plan. That was until a tiny idea popped into my practical-minded brain.

Over Christmas of 2016 we had been talking about finally moving our personal and business addresses to California. It had been almost two years since we had "chosen adventure," and while our original plan was to maybe move to other places for a year at a time, we loved California so much that we were ready to put down roots. As my logistical brain normally does, I was going over the address-change checklist in my head during a cross-country flight back to California after visiting with our families for the holidays.

This change of address would obviously require a lot of paperwork and registering with the proper state agencies, etc. My head was spinning with all the phone calls and signatures we would have to think about when I had a brilliant idea. Caroline and I were coming up on seven years together and if we followed through on our ten-year celebration plan, we were just going to have to jump through these hoops in a few short years again when Caroline changed her name. So—and let me just apologize ahead of time to all you romantics out there—I thought this would be a very practical time to save us some headaches and change our address AND Caroline's name at the same time. (You can imagine me coming to this very brilliant conclusion in my head, right?) Oh, and it's worth noting that we are a very progressive couple and Caroline didn't change her last name to my last name because of tradition, she opted to change it because her previous last name Winegeart was hard to spell, always pronounced wrong, and all-around just caused way more trouble than the shorter last name I'd finally picked: Zook.

As we walked out of the San Diego airport and I called us an Uber to drive back to our house, I decided to share my VERY brilliant idea with Caroline.

"Hey, I was thinking, since we're going to more permanently move our lives to California, maybe it's the perfect time to two-birds-one-stone this thing and just have you change your name, too?"

"Wait, what?" she looked genuinely confused.

"I'm just saying, since we agreed we're going to do the name change thing in a few years anyway, we could just take care of it when we become residents now."

She immediately started to laugh. "Wait . . . like you mean get married? Did you just propose while waiting for an Uber?"

Now, let me just interject and say we both had a pretty good laugh about this. I promise I was not trying to rob Caroline of a romantic life event. We had already discussed the idea of doing an unconventional, weird "mutual proposal" rather than the traditional get-down-on-one-knee thing (because . . . traditional) so this wasn't like a complete let down to something she had been dreaming of. But I know it was a genuinely surprising thought since we had both put the idea of getting married on the back burner.

During that Uber ride home, I watched Caroline go through a full range of emotions. She laughed. She stared out the window doing some mental calculation I couldn't quite pin down. She was surprised. She was in agreement. She was confused. (I imagine it's how she feels all the time in our relationship—hah!).

I knew it was a curveball, but in that moment I just felt ready. Now that I knew we both agreed we could create whatever version of a wedding (and a marriage) we wanted, one where we could own our weird, all I needed was that little practical nudge to show me there was no need to wait.

HAVING A MARRY-MENT

Over the course of the next few days and after many discussions about what our unconventional wedding could look like, we decided we wanted to elope (a fancy word for: get married by your damn selves!) and make it a super-small, special experience for us, not necessarily for everyone else. Taking that earlier article to heart, we were less concerned about a big party and a show, and more concerned about creating an experience where we could focus on each other and the future we were committing to.

So that's exactly what we did. On a random Tuesday, we got dressed up and exchanged vows on a cliff overlooking the ocean. There were flowers, and Caroline did wear a dress. But there weren't any distractions. Or cake. (We toasted with tequila and ate donuts as the sun went down.) We didn't even have an officiant—we made it "legal" the week before at the courthouse. There was no pressure or stress; just us and a memory that felt right. When talking about our special day with friends or family, we got in the habit of calling our custom ceremony a "marry-ment" since it wasn't quite an elopement or a wedding or a party. It was something we created just for us.

RELATIONSHIPS: THE ULTIMATE OWN YOUR WEIRD TEST

Our running joke with our families (who were as surprised as Caroline was—I think they assumed we'd never get married) was to theme our celebration "Practical Love" thanks to my paperwork proposal. That has come to be a sort of inside joke between us, and it reflects what is so important about doing relationships and love while owning your weird—it's about who YOU are and what you want, not what other people want for you. It's about not trying to make these important steps in life what you think they *should* be, but instead asking yourself what you *want* them to be.

A traditional, overly romantic wedding would have been us chasing down something because it's what we thought we were supposed to want and not what our relationship actually is, which is ultimately an equal partnership built on a foundation of friendship, humor, and a love of the unique things each of us brings to the table. (And yes, a mutual appreciation for all things practical and efficient.)

That's what worked for us. But it's not what might work for you. The most important thing is that you don't pressure yourself or your relationship to be something it's not. YOU get to decide what marriage is to you, what relationships will mean in your life, or if you even want to be in a relationship at all. You get to do relationships on your own terms and according to your values, your weirdness, and no one else's.

Chapter 12: "Own it!" recap and to-do item

- It's time to have your own marry-ment! Find a random stranger and have a weird wedding with them! Haha. Okay, sorry, I had to do it. The recap for this chapter and the takeaway I hope you'll "own" for your life is to ask yourself: am I making relationship decisions based on what I want or am I making decisions based on external forces that are against owning my weird? Deep philosophical question here, but an important one to answer, my friend.

CHAPTER 13

Friendships

When I was a kid, we moved around a lot. When I say a lot, I mean three high schools in four years. It felt like I played out the "new kid" scenario over and over again, wondering where to sit in the cafeteria, figuring out a way to strike up a conversation with another kid when I had no one else to talk to.

I share this because I'm sure these experiences have colored my perspective on making (and keeping) friends. For one, it taught me to be extremely discerning with my friendships. I came to expect we wouldn't stay in one place for too long so I was pretty cautious about getting attached. Looking back, I can see I kept most of my friends at arm's length. When I did finally make close friendships that were deeper than surface level, it meant even more to me because it meant I was risking having to say goodbye.

That said, moving also taught me I was actually okay without having a bunch of friends. Keeping in touch was much harder before the days of texting and Facebook, so when we moved and a friendship just sort of faded in the rearview mirror, I learned that the world actually didn't come crashing down. Over time I developed confidence in my ability to make at least one new friend wherever we were going.

The Own Your Weird approach is about choosing to live your life through the lens of your own uniqueness, not what society or anyone else tells you. This applies to friendships as well. I've come to develop my own ideas about what friendship means to me and how I choose which friendships to cultivate in my life.

THE ROLE OF FRIENDSHIP

What does it mean to be a friend? This is a question that every person could answer differently, which is exactly what makes it a question worth asking. I'm not one of those people that believes a friend is just someone you've known a long time. For me, friendship is much more intentional than that. I believe the role of a friend is first and foremost to support you. This doesn't mean they can't challenge you or offer thoughtful feedback about your decisions, but ultimately I believe a friend should encourage you first *before* doubting you. To give you the benefit of the doubt because they know you on a deeper level.

FRIENDS AS PEER-MENTORS

I don't have mentors in my life. I know that's a bold statement (did you expect anything different by this point?) but it's the truth. I realized as an adult and entrepreneur, I want friends whom I can see as peer-mentors. People who are also in the trenches, owning their weird in their own right, challenging norms and inspiring me to do the same. That's why it's so important to me I only keep friends in my life who understand the importance of questioning convention, embracing their uniqueness, and wanting to grow and get better as people.

When I think about what I look for in a friend, I want people who inspire me and motivate me. Some people choose to surround themselves with people wildly different from them. That's cool—I just haven't found those relationships to be the most fruitful ones for me. Of course I don't want a bunch of Jason clones running around telling me how great I am (although, if Amazon decides to come out with those I don't know if I could resist buying, with free next-day shipping!) What I mean is that, for me, there needs to be an underlying foundation of like-mindedness. **Our opinions and choices can be different, but our values need to be similar.**

There's a very famous quote from the author and entrepreneur Jim Rohn that I'm sure you've heard before, but it bears repeating: "You are the average of the five people you spend the most time with." And it's absolutely true. For me, it's not just having people that will show up for me. It's also about being surrounded by people that will make me better.

THE RIGHT NUMBER OF FRIENDS

Thanks to social media, we live in an age where the subconscious consensus seems to be the more friends the better. But I disagree. Much like incorporating minimalism into my life when it comes to possessions, I apply the same principles to relationships. More is not necessarily better. It's about the quality of friendships and the value each one brings to my life.

As I write this, I'm counting how many people I consider close friends, by which I mean people I can call in a moment's notice, who support me before doubting me, and who feel I do the same for them. The number I came to: eight.

Is eight friends "enough?" Shouldn't I have WAY more friends? Heck, I have social media accounts with thousands of followers, certainly there are more than eight people I could lean on if need be. While that may be true, the truth is that these are the eight people I've chosen to invest in and who've chosen to invest in me.

The number doesn't matter. If anything, I think it's time we recognize our own limitations as people. In friendship, you have to be willing to give, to listen, to show up, to cultivate that relationship intentionally. If you try to give yourself to dozens of friendships on a regular basis, what are you giving up and are you giving all you could?

Whether you have eight friends or eight hundred, the most important thing is to ask yourself: are the people I'm surrounding myself with aligned with my values, my beliefs; do they embrace my weirdness; and are they willing to show up for me if I need them?

I for one like having a small group of people that I am responsible for. If I believe friendship asks us to drop everything and show up for a friend in need, I can't do that with a hundred people. But I can feel good about knowing I could do it for eight.

The right number of friends is the number that allows you to stay connected in the terms you define for what friendship means to you.

TOXIC FRIENDSHIPS

If I were to ask you, "Hey person reading this right now, do you think you have toxic friendships?" Your immediate answer might be, "No Jason, my friends are all great people who love me and only want me to be happy!" But is that really the truth?

Sometimes a toxic friendship is hard to spot, especially if you've spent years with that person in your life. But if you have someone who constantly discourages you and your ideas, or makes you feel bad for wanting to own your weird or step outside your comfort zone, or someone who makes every interaction about them . . . these are things that can have a negative impact on your self-confidence without you even knowing.

The people you surround yourself with can lift you up or they can drag you down. If you're the average of the five people you spend the most time around, don't you want people who are going to bring your average up?

TOXIC COMPLACENCY

I've been lucky enough in my life that I've never encountered a friend that I would describe as toxic, but I have encountered friendships with people who have what I call "toxic complacency." If toxic friends can be hard to spot because of a blind spot, toxic complacency friends are ten times harder to spot. This is the kind of person who might be unhappy or dissatisfied with their life but they seem perfectly content to stay in their dissatisfaction. They complain about everything and yet they refuse to change anything. Sometimes you wonder if they actually like being miserable.

It took me a long time to realize that these people could be weighing me down, too. I had a roommate in the early days of IWearYourShirt (IWYS) whom we'll call Kevin (everyone say hello to Kevin!). Kevin was, as far as roommates go, fantastic. He was neat and tidy. He always paid rent on time. And, we'd shared a bunch of common interests: working out, playing basketball, and a love of random terrible movies.

One thing we didn't have in common was our career choice. I don't remember exactly what Kevin did from 9 to 5, all I remember is that he drove forty-five minutes to and from work to get to his job, and never once did I hear him say, "Man, work was awesome today!" I think after the third or fourth day of living together I gave up entirely on asking him about his workday, as it was never fun for either of us.

All of that being said, Kevin was a really nice guy. I distinctly remember, though, the day Kevin came home and I wanted to tell him about IWYS. I was so excited to share the idea with someone. After looking pretty confused he just said: "Why don't you just keep doing what's already working with your design company?" Now, that's a perfectly reasonable thing to think (for people who aren't obsessed with owning their weird), but for me it became painfully obvious that our friendship probably wasn't going to last long-term. Kevin was okay with the status quo, even if the status quo wasn't that great.

I used to spend the majority of my time with the Kevins of the world. While good-natured people, Kevins are okay with living a mediocre life, working at a soul-sucking 9 to 5 job, buying into the pressures of society, and refusing to take risks of any kind (or share vulnerable moments of failure). When I was living in my beige stage, having Kevin as a friend was fine. But I realized leaving that monotone life behind meant I needed to leave the Kevins in my life behind as well.

PROXIMITY PEOPLE

You may have heard the term "slow fade" before. It's typically used when two people are dating, and one party decides they're done dating but doesn't want to rip the Band-Aid off. Instead, they start ignoring calls, texts, emails, and they slowly fade out of the other person's life. Hence: slow fade. This is what I started doing as my entrepreneurial career continued after 2009. I started to slow fade away from all my existing friendships. I didn't make some big stink about it and berate them for not supporting my dreams. That wouldn't have been fair to them because our relationship wasn't built on the foundation that I was a dreamer who needed supporting.

Instead, most of my friendships were built on a foundation of college acquaintance, my 9 to 5 job, playing sports, really just anything to do with proximity. And as the famous math equation by Einstein goes: $f + \pi \neq ©$. Oh, I'm being told I just made that up. What I meant was: person + proximity ≠ friendship. Just because people are near you or around you on a daily basis, doesn't mean they'll make good friends.

What did I do besides slow fade "friends" out of my life? I started to ask myself what a friend would really mean to me. I wondered if I had to keep in constant contact with a person to consider them a friend. I, because I'm analytical, thought about what a true friend would mean to me instead of just allowing anyone to jump into my friendship circle (wild concept!). As I was evolving as a person, my idea of what a friend meant was, too.

I'd be lying if I said I had it figured out right away in 2009. Instead, I went through some "seasonal friendships," as Caroline calls them. I had friends who were fighting the same life and business battles I was. It was great to call them friends for a few years, while we were going through similar life events. But eventually the majority of those folks would create new values that didn't align with my burgeoning ones. I even found friends by proximity who did match up to the stuff that mattered to me in my life, but when I moved away from them, the relationships fizzled out (and that's okay!). Instead of worrying about keeping a friend forever (because, BFF), I've come to appreciate the role a certain person plays at a certain time in my life. And hopefully vice versa!

Just because I had access to lots of connections through social media and in-person social circles, it didn't actually mean I had lots of friends. And guess what? Who cares how many friends you have?? You can't cash in the amount of friendships you have to get more happiness coins at the Carnival of Life. (That does sound like an episode of Black Mirror though, doesn't it?) I'm incredibly happy to call a small group of people my friends. I'm happy to know that, no matter what, these folks are going to be stand by and support me. But I also realize that we may part ways in a few years, and that's okay, too. We're supposed to evolve. We're supposed to change. We're not the same people we were before, so we may not need the same people around us anymore.

Chapter 13: "Own it!" recap and to-do item

- Is there one friend in your life whom you know fits into the toxic complacency category? Someone who makes you feel bad for owning your weird? Maybe it's time to sit them down and have an honest conversation about how they treat you and your unique ideas? Or maybe it's time to give yourself permission to perform your own "slow fade" of that relationship so you can make room for someone who supports your weirdness more and aligns with your values?

CHAPTER 14

Working to Live, Not Living to Work

I used to believe that being "busy" was a good thing. I used to wear my hours worked per week like a badge of honor. Working sixty- to one-hundred-hour weeks meant I was a *real* entrepreneur, a *real* business owner, someone that other people would respect for prioritizing work over everything else. Being busy meant I wasn't just talking about my crazy ideas; it meant I was getting out there and doing something about them.

For the first few years of IWearYourShirt, I didn't take a single day off. Every weekday and weekend I had a sponsor, made a YouTube video, etc. I actually distinctly remember being proud of working weekends because it meant I was getting a leg up on the majority of people who were only working weekdays. That thought was a direct reflection of my competitive outlook on business at the time.

I will say, making my whole life revolve around my business served me well for a few years. There's no doubt those hours of hard work definitely paid off. IWearYourShirt did get all kinds of press and had a very profitable run for a while, reaching what you might traditionally call "success" and providing me with the financial means to live a great life. Except, that is, working so much didn't leave me much time to actually *enjoy* that great life.

This "hustle" mindset spilled over into my work post-IWearYourShirt. I felt like I was starting over from square one, and I was anxious to prove to myself (and everyone else) that I wasn't a one-trick pony. I spent late nights and weekends working, shoving important things to the back burner like health, travel, and rest.

As time went on and projects after IWearYourShirt went well, I started to reflect on the mistakes I'd made that I didn't want to repeat. Rearranging my life around my work at all costs was the biggest one. I thought to myself, *What is this all* for, *anyway?* What's the hard work and long nights and squeezing every last moment of productivity out of each day *for?* So other people would think I was successful? To make as much money as possible? (I was already making enough to live well.)

I realized I was working so hard for this goal off in the distance that looked like financial security, being able to travel, having free time to do whatever I wanted. And yet, if I wanted them, weren't those things available to me NOW? So again, what was it all *for?* Similar to my feelings about retirement, I didn't want to spend all my waking hours "saving up" my enjoyment for later on in life. Instead, I wanted to find a way to bring more enjoyment into my daily life in the present.

That's when I had a radical thought. Instead of scheduling my life around my work, what if I scheduled my work around my life?

What if instead of living to work all the time, I focused on working to LIVE?

What if I used my business as a *tool* to fuel the life I wanted to live?

It sounds like such a simple reframing, but the results were actually pretty drastic for me. Here's how the Working to Live approach (as Caroline and I started calling it) changed the way I operate on a daily basis:

- **Scheduling life first on my calendar, then work**—I started to think about what a perfect day would look like: Waking up without an alarm. Enjoying my morning coffee ritual. Making time for exercise. Doing some writing. Having some sort of adventure with my wife (even if that was just a mid-morning action flick featuring Dwayne "The Rock" Johnson). Whatever activities I wanted in my life, I put those in my calendar first. Using the time slots that were left over, I scheduled my work hours.

- **Making my "badge of honor" my ability to live out daily values**—No longer was it about how many hours or weekends I could work. I started measuring my own success based on how much living I was doing. As long as my business was making enough money to sustain a lifestyle where I had the freedom to take time off and not work every waking moment, I was succeeding.

- **Embracing free time without guilt**—For the first few days of prioritizing the life I wanted first, there was definitely a feeling of guilt. It felt like cheating. Can I really do this? Am I *allowed* to do it? Shouldn't I at least work four to five hours every day, if not more? I can't possibly bake homemade biscuits, go for a hike, laze around reading, and THEN fit an hour or two of work in my day, can I? It took some getting used to, but eventually I went back to that question above: what is it all for? Life should be lived now, not later.

FEWER HOURS, MORE PRODUCTIVITY

A funny thing happens when you force yourself to have fewer hours you can work in a day: You actually get more done! You stop distracting yourself. You stop allowing yourself to wander off around the Internet. You crave getting back to the life stuff that makes you really happy, and you become ruthless with accomplishing the work that actually matters. Shifting my mindset from business first to life first actually made me more productive in the hours I chose to work.

Giving yourself clear boundaries and limited chunks of work during the day also helps you become extremely focused and discerning when it comes to strategizing for your business. You become hyper-focused on what is contributing to the overall health of your business because you know you only have a limited number of hours in the day to move the needle. Instead of losing yourself in social media for an hour, you find yourself actually making progress on the projects that will bring you direct revenue.

I DON'T WANT MORE; I JUST WANT ENOUGH

As I made my transition from workaholic (a.k.a.: hustle bro, who was always busy), I started to look at the people around me and what they were searching for. I remember I visited a group of entrepreneurs who had come together for a weekend "mastermind retreat." A friend who was a part of the group asked me if I wanted to swing by to chat business, and I said sure. I knew a couple of the people from Twitter and other Internet things and was genuinely excited to meet them in real life (whoa, imagine that!).

After some idle chitchat, the group sat down at a big table and we all went around talking about the various states of our businesses. For every person, the focus turned to the things they wanted to grow, the areas of their lives they wanted to expand, and the milestones they had been dreaming of. (This doesn't surprise you, right? Most of us, especially entrepreneurs, spend our mental energy preoccupied with what's next.)

One by one, I listened to each person talk about more. More money. More customers. More employees. It was always more. I'm sure they didn't realize it, but that word was all I heard in everything they were sharing.

When the conversation came around to me, a thought hit me like a bolt of lightning. I said something to the effect of, "This is probably going to come off wrong, but I feel like I've made it. I don't need more of anything. I'm right where I want to be—and I probably have the least revenue, customers, employee, of anyone here." I'm not going to say you could hear a pin drop, but it was pretty awkward for a few moments after that. Then one guy spoke up and said, "that's awesome man, good for you," and they quickly moved on to the next person.

I left that little get-together realizing I was in a place in business and life where I felt like I had *enough*. We were renting a home where we could look out over the Pacific Ocean every day. I had free time during the day to do whatever I wanted. No one was telling us what to do or where to be when. I could shut my laptop at any moment and the world wouldn't come crashing down. We had some savings in case of emergencies. We had a small, but dedicated group of customers who liked what we were putting out into the world (and who were great people—hello WAIMers!). Plus the ability to travel and have new adventures.

That was more than enough.

I've come to realize the idea of *enough* scares people, whether you're a single person working for yourself or a mom supporting a family. Focusing on having enough feels restrictive. It feels limiting. It contradicts every hedonistic instinct we as humans have. When you're so conditioned to constantly look ahead to what's next, it's uncomfortable to look around and consider enjoying what you have now. It goes against everything you hear about, read about, and are taught in life and business.

More is better! You'll be happier if you just make more money! Get more followers! Hire more people! MORE! But the times in my life when I narrowed in on trying to aim for more are the times I've been most stressed, overworked, and least happy.

Changing my focus from more to enough the past few years has been critical for my overall happiness and enjoyment in my work. It feels like I used to be on a treadmill, constantly running with the idea that the treadmill would eventually land me in HappyTown. The faster I ran, the quicker I thought I'd arrive at the proverbial finish line. But after that awkward statement I made to a group of strangers, I felt like I jumped off the treadmill completely and started walking around at my own pace. There wasn't a finish line or a town I was trying to get to. And sometimes I'm not even walking at all. Sure, it feels weird to not see a business grow "up and to the right" in some linear way and to get accustomed to enjoying things as they are without chasing after something else, but that's only because I've been conditioned for thirty-plus years to think that "more" was the right way.

Now my only concern is to regularly check in with myself (and Caroline) and make sure that my values are still well-defined. As long as my business is serving a life that reflects those values, that's enough for me.

Now I want to pose that same question to you: what if you stopped striving for more? More money. More customers. More notoriety. More, more, more.

What if, instead, you started focusing on enough? *Enough* money to live the life you want right now. *Enough* customers to sustain your business. *Enough* notoriety . . . (heck, maybe no notoriety at all as a focus?).

The problem with focusing on more is that it's a sliding scale. You set a goal, you reach it, and the goal line moves. It leaves you feeling perpetually in a state of lacking. Focusing on enough forces you to get specific about defining what success means to you. It allows you to set a goal, reach it, and then feel the contentment and satisfaction of that.

SOFTWARE SIDE HUSTLE

Owning your weird doesn't just apply to what my goals are; it also applies to how I choose to run my businesses as well. For example, take the software company that I co-founded, Teachery.

As I mentioned earlier, this company wasn't born out of a desire to create a startup or hunt down funding. It started as a piece of software I built for myself and some friends because I saw a need for an online course platform that was simple, user-friendly, and affordable. I had no idea it was going to become a Software as a Service (SaaS) business. I didn't know the first thing about creating software or getting customers for it. But, I figured it out step-by-step. I carved out tiny chunks of time and, along with my co-founder Gerlando, we improved the software little by little.

Gerlando and I were in complete alignment from the very beginning: Teachery would be a side project (or side hustle, depending on the popular term of the moment) for both of us. We weren't focused on getting funding. We didn't care about making gobs of money every month. We didn't want to concern ourselves with competing with anyone else or any other course platform.

This intentional slow-growth approach allowed us to never get too stressed out about building our first software product together. I was able to get us a handful of paying customers, many of whom still use Teachery to this day years later.

Teachery's stats aren't going to blow you away: we made $13,000 in the first year (hah!). But, there's been steady, sustainable, pain-free growth over the years. In 2017, Teachery netted over $84,000 in revenue—all without ever focusing on marketing or growth. In fact, from the beginning of building Teachery, it was my goal to only ever grow the customer base and revenue through word-of-mouth marketing. Talk about owning your weird, right? More important, we've given our customers a platform that allowed them to sell $2,500,000+ in course sales and create incredible opportunities for themselves (one of the things I'm most proud of!).

No one told us we could build Teachery. There was no blueprint for it. We followed our own weird intentional path. We carved out time and energy and built Teachery in our spare time. We've always avoided burning ourselves out because we aren't chasing some huge arbitrary financial goal (read: more). Teachery has been and will continue to be an awesome piece of my entrepreneurial arsenal that personifies owning my weird in business.

I wanted to share this example to show you that you get to decide how you want to run your business. You get to choose how big or small, what your goals are, if you grow or not. You don't have to "play entrepreneur" or make decisions based on what some Silicon Valley startup would do. You can build the business that aligns with your lifestyle and write your own blueprint just like you can with every other aspect of your life.

BUSINESS ESSENTIALISM
· ·

In my list of books I most often recommend to people, *Essentialism* by Greg McKeown is way up there. It's a simple but incredibly effective shift in thinking. Instead of allowing your focus to go in a multitude of directions with your focus stretched thin, it suggests focusing in on the most essential and most impactful thing. It's the idea of pursuing *fewer, but better* things. Quality over quantity. You can apply this idea to just about anything: possessions (hence, minimalism), ideas, projects, friends, etc.

One of the most surprising ways this advice has made its way into my life is in my business. After years of exploration and experimentation, I've asked myself how I can strip the excess away and narrow in on only the most valuable aspects of my business (both for me, as the owner, and for my customers.)

Take my BuyMyFuture project, for example. (Don't remember what that project was? I'll save you the time. BuyMyFuture is when I bundled together all my projects and courses and sold them for one price, including anything I would ever create in the future for the rest of my life!)

At the time of conceiving BuyMyFuture in 2015, I couldn't stop thinking that I had eight-plus products I was trying to sell, with even more in the works. I loved the process of creating those projects, but really disliked the repetitive anguish of promoting, marketing, and supporting them on an ongoing basis. Each project brought about its own new challenges and sustaining each one further fragmented my attention.

The idea for BuyMyFuture was my solution to that problem. (*Fewer* projects, but a *better* overall experience.) If I could promote, market, and sell ONE project, it would free up a ton of mental energy and time. Plus, BuyMyFuture was the ultimate value proposition for a customer: they get all the current stuff, all the future projects, and never have to make a purchasing decision again.

Essentialism is also extremely helpful if you're building anything where you get feedback and requests from your customers. You can put the things they ask for through this essentialism filter: *is spending time on this one request going to make a greater impact for all our customers, or should this wait for more people to ask for it?* It felt difficult for me at first to adopt this line of thinking. I wanted to take care of every request for every customer. What you don't realize is you're spreading your energy and effort so thin that you can't make a bigger overall impact (that could lead to even happier customers who help spread the word about your business for you). And just to be clear, when it comes to customer requests and features, I always reply to customers and say they've been heard and considered, but that we're working on XYZ feature instead and we'll try to get to their concerns.

As creators, many of us fall prey to shiny-object syndrome. You know what I'm talking about, right? You have a plan. You know what you should be working on. Then . . . Boom! A shiny object comes along that wants to pull you in an entirely new direction. It's new, it's exciting, it doesn't require any discipline! But by having the core concept of essentialism in your mind at all times, you can evaluate if that shiny object makes sense for where you are currently focusing your energy, or if that object should be put somewhere for safekeeping to be looked at later. (Pro-tip: I keep all my shiny objects—a.k.a. ideas—in a Google Doc. When it's time to focus on something new, I come back to them. But do I ever come back to them? No! That's because I shouldn't be focusing on those shiny objects anyway. I should be focusing on bringing the shine back to my existing projects!)

With every business I own or think about starting, I use the principles of essentialism to evaluate where I should be spending my time. Yes, it's important to take care of the little things, but it's also important to make sure you're putting your energy in the right place to help build a great product for your customer and a business that provides the life you want.

Chapter 14: "Own it!" recap and to-do item

- There are many things I could challenge you with for this "Own it!" but the one I think may make the BIGGEST impact on your life is to visit wanderingaimfully.com/working and to go through the Working to Live exercises we've created (that have radically impacted and improved our lives!). Don't think you can schedule your life first on your calendar? It's time to test that assumption, my friend!

OWN IT!

CREATING YOUR OWN YOUR WEIRD BLUEPRINT IN BUSINESS AND LIFE

Alright, alright, enough about me. Now that you've seen some of the ways I interpret the Own Your Weird mantra in my life, I want to talk about how you can start using it to work toward the life you want TODAY. If you've decided you're ready to scrap the existing blueprint that isn't working for you and create your own from here on out, where do you start? This last section aims to answer that question and these last few chapters are full of the *practical* lessons that are essential to really owning your weird.

CHAPTER 15

Show Up Authentically and Consistently

When you're owning your weird—especially in business—people won't always get it right away. But there is a way to make sure people pay attention long enough for the right ones to come to understand what you're trying to do.

The two critical things you'll need when building a business (or living a life, for that matter) that can help you stand out are *authenticity* and *consistency*. Each one has its individual merits, but the real magic is when you use them together. Like peanut butter and jelly, they're fine solo, but together they're a national treasure (and not the Nicholas Cage movie kind, although, go back and watch those movies, they're fun!).

Authenticity means showing up on the outside in the same way that you feel on the inside. It's being yourself—your true self. Consistency means showing up over and over again on a predictable basis. When you create work that is sincere and authentic to you, and you do it reliably for long enough, it doesn't matter how differently you decide to do things—the right people WILL find you.

AUTHENTICITY

First let's talk about authenticity. Being yourself—showing up in the world in a way that is true to who you are and not what other people want for you—is the core concept of owning your weird. I hope that's pretty clear by now. But why is this so powerful? It's because people can feel sincerity. They can sense truth, and they trust it.

People can also feel it when you're desperately trying to keep up an appearance or tell them what they want to hear. If they come to discover this, you lose that trust that's so crucial for building a relationship with an audience or a customer base.

When I started writing weekly articles on my previous website JasonDoesStuff.com, I made the conscious decision early on to write from a place of authenticity, not from a place of authority.

For years while I ran IWearYourShirt (2009–2013), I felt like I couldn't be REAL, honest, and authentic on a daily basis. Because I was physically representing a company on my chest every day, I had to be "on." Everything had to look perfect because if it didn't, I could potentially make a company look bad. Trying to keep up a facade is exhausting and unsustainable.

So as I started to send my weekly articles to *The Action Army* (even the name of my email list owned my weird), I started to push my own authenticity boundaries. I started to be more honest and pull back the curtain when things hadn't gone perfectly. And a funny thing started to happen. I had thought sharing in this way would push people away, but instead, my writing resonated with many more people. And that resonance with my authenticity is what kept people coming back every Monday, curious at what I would share next.

The idea of authenticity goes back to embracing your weirdness. You have to have the courage to actually share yourself with people. Yes, being vulnerable or different comes with the risk of people being turned off or opening yourself up for criticism, but that risk is often rewarded with a deeper emotional connection. If you can find customers that trust you and like you for exactly who you are (imperfections and all), they are way more likely to stick with you through the twists and turns of your business journey. Think about the people you follow or look up to, would you categorize them as people who proactively own their weird? I know I do!

YOU MAY LOSE SOME PEOPLE

When I was starting over after IWearYourShirt, I had an email list of twenty-five thousand people left over from that business. Unsure of how to transition them to the next chapter of my business journey, I sent a heartfelt email that was more real than I'd been in a long time, telling them about my new venture and asking them to opt back in to this new brand (JasonDoesStuff) that would represent a more authentic version of myself.

Do you want to know how stunning being authentic can be? Out of those twenty-five thousand people, only four hundred of them opted in to my newsletter, *The Action Army*. The ten thousand people who opened the email but didn't opt in decided the real, weird me wasn't the one they bargained for, and I had to be okay with that.

But, this is where I had to shift my perspective, as you will, too, if you double down on authenticity. Sure, thousands of people said no thanks, but four hundred people raised their hand and said YES to following my journey.

Whatever change you want to make toward a more authentic life or business, it may only be forty people or four people that raise their hand to support you in that. But that's okay. **Life is not about how many people we can get to say "yes" to us. Life is about finding the *right* people who will say "yes" time and time again.**

WHAT DOES AUTHENTICITY LOOK LIKE FOR YOU?

Let's shift gears and get specific about what changes you can or need to make to show up more authentically—changes that you may be avoiding due to the discomfort that can come with revealing the real you and actively owning your weird.

I'd like to challenge you to write down, right here in this book, one place in your life where you know you aren't being 100 percent authentic.

_____

(Write it down on the line above. Don't skip ahead! If you're on Kindle, grab a piece of paper or a Post-It note and write it down, too.)

Now, look at what you wrote and ask yourself: WHY are you not being more authentic in this area of your life? Don't shortchange yourself on this answer. Be honest. Is it because you're afraid of rejection from someone? Maybe a family member, friends, or existing customers? My guess is yes. Get specific about who that person is or who those people are. Ask yourself if the opinions of those people are worth more than the freedom of being yourself.

Let's get even more specific and apply this to your business. What is something you're currently doing in your business that doesn't truly align with how you want to be doing things? I'll ask this another way: what's something you're doing in your business that you're doing because it works for other people and you think you have to do it, but it doesn't quite feel right to you?

_____

(Again: Write it down!)

Here are some examples from myself and fellow entrepreneurs. Some of these things might be "industry standard" or disproportionately effective, but some of them don't align with who I am deep down.

- Hosting bait-and-switch webinars to sell a digital product or course

- Using discounts and promotions to try to attract customers

- Putting ALL the pop-ups on your website to try to get more email subscribers/customers

- Sending automated emails or not doing email marketing at all

- Trying to scale your company with more employees/clients/customers

- Posting perfectly posed photos on social media to look like you have it all together

Those are just a small handful of things I see happening all the time. And I'm not saying there's anything inherently wrong with any of those tactics. It's just that many business owners use these tactics because they think they have to, when really it's up to you to decide how you want to run your business and what feels good.

CONSISTENCY

....

Being yourself is critical, but what's even more critical is being yourself over and over again on a regular basis. That last part is essential if you want to build a business that owns your weird and excites you to work on it every day. Whereas in life you can write your own rules and it doesn't matter if people get it or not, business is a bit different because you need customers to run a profitable business. People have to get it or you have no revenue. Consistency is that missing piece.

Consistency is important because it allows you to hone your voice, get better at a skill, and again, build trust with an audience.

When you're owning your weird, you're creating your own blueprint for personal success from scratch. That means you're flying blind in the beginning and you're bound to make a few missteps. Many people try to "out-think" this part of the process in an effort to avoid those mistakes, when truthfully the best way to conquer them is to move *through* them. That's what consistency does for you. It allows you to keep taking a swing over and over and over until you finally get a hit.

Are you trying to become a better writer? Then you need to write more consistently and with less judgment.

Are you trying to become better at selling/sales? Then you need to try to sell more and learn what works and what doesn't (and become okay with hearing no).

Are you trying to hire better people? Then you need to learn what actually motivates people and what steps you can put in place that empower an employee to enjoy the work they do and be a great worker.

When I made the decision to start writing consistently on JasonDoesStuff.com to help grow my business(es), I knew my early writing was going to be bad. But, I also knew that in my previous experience filming a daily YouTube video, I went from a cringeworthy, unwatchable, horrendously embarrassing first video to videos that thousands of people would enjoy one thousand videos later.

Repetition builds mastery and confidence. Not only do you get better at what you're doing but you get braver as well with consistency.

WHAT'S STOPPING YOU FROM BEING MORE CONSISTENT?

Just about any marketing tactic I can think of requires consistency to be effective. Whether it's content marketing like articles, videos, or posts on Instagram, or whether it's something more fundamental like customer service, consistency is a prerequisite. Yet I find so many business owners struggle with this.

I want you to think of ONE thing in your life that you've struggled to stay consistent with. Now ask yourself, what's stopping you?

Is it that you don't "know what you're doing?" Is it that you're looking for the right blueprint to follow or that you think you need fancy equipment? Go back to our lessons from Chapter 6 and challenge each of these answers. Are they real barriers or just assumptions-based excuses?

Consistency takes discipline, courage, and effort. Showing up on a regular basis, even when you don't feel like it, means learning to combat mental roadblocks, procrastination battles, and avoidance tactics. But, like many things we do consistently in our lives, many behaviors get easier to show up for over time: brushing your teeth, bathing, putting on underwear, being a reasonably nice human being to other human beings. If you can find a way to overcome those barriers to consistency earlier on, eventually showing up isn't quite as hard.

BUILDING AN AUDIENCE WITH AUTHENTICITY AND CONSISTENCY

Now let's talk about these crucial elements in terms of specific tactics. Let's apply the authenticity and consistency combo in order to build an audience for your business—differently.

In today's business environment, before you can ever get sales, you have to get attention. That means attracting an audience that cares about what you have to say or what product/service you're selling. In my opinion, this authenticity and consistency combo is the magic combination to get you there.

SHOW UP AUTHENTICALLY AND CONSISTENTLY

Now let's get practical: identify one action you think you need to take to get your work out there: Is your work your writing? Is your work the art you create and want to sell? Or is your work the code you've been learning in your free time but want to start charging other people for as a freelance developer? Whatever that thing is that you do or make, focus in on one way you can show up authentically and consistently. Then follow these three basic steps:

1. **Establish a schedule.** The first thing I did when I committed to start writing consistently was to establish a schedule for myself. From my previous experience filming a daily YouTube video, I knew that writing and publishing a daily article was out of the question. A weekly schedule felt more doable, plus, Seth Godin is about the only person I know that sends a daily email that people actually enjoy/care about. I decided I would send out my weekly article on Mondays, for no other reason than this: I wanted to make people's Mondays suck a little bit less. That was the honest reason for picking Monday morning as my scheduled article time (had nothing to do with industry statistics on email opens, etc.).

2. **Come up with a concise way to communicate your uniqueness. This is your authenticity magnet.** The second thing I did was sit down with Caroline and come up with some sort of hook that would attract people to sign up to receive my weekly emails. At the time, I had already amassed an email list of twenty-five thousand for my IWearYourShirt business, but I had learned from previous mistakes that I wasn't going to just start sending that list of people my weekly articles. My website is called JasonDoesStuff, but I didn't want to simply create the "JasonDoesStuff Newsletter." That's not sexy. That's not unique. That's not different. The more Caroline and I chatted, the more we settled on the fact that I wanted not only to help Mondays suck less (maybe "Make Mondays Suck Less!" is a future newsletter name) but that I wanted to help people take action. That was something I had to really start embracing about myself. I am very good at getting things done and my writing voice tends to have an actionable energy to it. This is how *The Action Army* was born. This is an example of me building authenticity right into the name of my newsletter in order to create a magnet, attracting readers and customers who want to take more action in their lives.

3. **Put in the work.** The third, and most important, thing I did was I sat in the chair, I wrote, and I hit publish. I accepted the fact that perfect writing wouldn't just fall out of the sky and into a Google Doc. I had to force the writing out of me and had to be willing to share less-than-perfect articles. And I did. Starting with my very first article titled "Think Reinvention—Not Resolutions."

As of the writing of this book, I consistently wrote an article to *The Action Army* every Monday for nearly four years. I sent over 130 articles, each one on a Monday, and none of them were ever perfect. In fact, there were many times I was embarrassed to hit send. But I did it anyway. Because, much like brushing your teeth, when you do something that's good for you with consistency, it also builds momentum and confidence that you are taking care of business.

As you've read this book, there may be areas of your life or business that you want to apply the Own Your Weird mindset to, but you're still scared to take that leap and embrace your weirdness so you can stand out. If you can make sure that you employ authenticity and consistency when you decide to carve out your own path and show the real you, you will be so much more likely to have the right people "get it" and pay attention.

Chapter 15: "Own it!" recap and to-do item

- There were two areas in this chapter where you were supposed to, MadLib-style, fill in the blank with your answers. You didn't do that yet, did you? How'd I know? Book authors have magical powers and I'm actually watching you through each page of this book . . . mwahaha! Kidding, kidding. Or am I? No I am. Anyhoo, go back a few pages and fill out the two fill-in-the-blank spots and answer the questions associated. Then holler "I OWNED IT!" so I can hear you through the pages.

CHAPTER 16

You Don't Get What You Don't Ask For

Forging your own path will often require you to go out on a limb and make an ask of another person. That could mean asking employees to support you when you pursue a new and weird idea. That could mean asking customers to give you money for something that's never been done before. That could mean asking people in positions of power to take a chance on you or give you an opportunity.

Here's one of the most powerful statements I have learned to be true as a person trying to build a business and live a life that is outside the norm: **You don't get what you don't ask for.**

Think about that statement for a moment. What have you missed out on in life or business because you simply didn't ask for what you wanted? Making an ask is such a simple concept, yet so many people are afraid of being rejected so they never take that leap.

Most people's default setting is to wait around for opportunities to come to them. They wait for someone to choose them or present them with an offer that will get them closer to what they want. But asking is about shifting the power back into your own hands and saying you can go out there and create those opportunities for yourself. It's about not rejecting yourself before someone else can. Making any kind of ask feels strange and vulnerable at first, but asking gets easier over time.

ARE YOU MAKING MONEY
OR JUST GETTING PAID?

This idea—that you could create your own opportunities by asking, rather than just waiting for them to come to you—was cemented into my head from the first $13 I ever made.

IWearYourShirt had just launched to crickets on the first day (and those crickets apparently didn't have money, the cheap jerks). In a bit of a panic, I started emailing friends and family to share the website with them. (Yes, it's embarrassing that this hadn't occurred to me before, but remember this was my first big idea and I was learning the simplest lessons in marketing the hard way.)

Those few emails to friends and family weren't sales pitches. They were just friendly hellos, accompanied by a request to check out or share this crazy T-shirt wearing business I had come up with. I remember feeling so nervous about sending the link to them, knowing a few of them were skeptical when I first shared the idea with them, but I also remember thinking to myself: "If I don't tell people about this idea, how in the world do I expect them to find it?"

A few of the email recipients actually took pity on me and deposited money into my PayPal account via the fancy buttons on the website link I'd sent them. After the first day of sending emails one by one, I had made (brace yourself) . . . $13.

I'll give you a moment to pick yourself up off the floor. Are you okay? You are? Great.

I know $13 doesn't sound like much, and most people would probably be disappointed with a first day of sales coming in at less than the cost of a movie these days, but I had the opposite reaction. Those were thirteen dollars that I *made* myself—essentially, out of thin air. I had an idea . . . I created a sales proposition offering something of value . . . I had a way for people to pay me . . . and money went into my account.

I'm going to steal this wonderful sentiment from Caroline (mostly because she's the better writer of the two of us), but it taught me that **there's a difference between making money and getting paid.** Making money is active; getting paid is passive. Making money says you can create your own opportunities for financial gain; getting paid says you have to wait around for someone else to deem you worthy of it.

That first day of IWearYourShirt taught me that I didn't need to show up to a job and get a paycheck. I could *write* the paychecks. I could create my own opportunities. I could *make* money. I just had to be willing to go out on a limb and make an ask.

But . . . making money requires more courage than getting paid. Making money is usually in the Own Your Weird camp, and as you know by now, rejection is a part of walking that path.

THE CONSEQUENCES OF ASKING

The idea of making money is empowering, sure, but it's also a lot more vulnerable than getting paid. Why? Because if you're making an ask, you're opening yourself up to rejection—a feeling that most of us fear and are desperate to avoid.

There's a character in Pixar's movie *Inside Out* named Fear. Fear is a jerk. He shows up at the worst times and dominates all other emotions whenever he so chooses. He keeps us from living our lives to the fullest extent, whether that means dropping off a cliff (with safety gear, duh) or asking someone to buy the thing we've made.

In certain circumstances of my life, I'm happy that Fear exists. He keeps me from climbing six-foot ladders. He keeps me from looking over the railing in a mall (I get chills just thinking about this). Without Fear, I'd make some pretty bad decisions and end up doing stupidly dangerous stuff (and yes, I consider climbing a six-foot ladder hideously dangerous).

But in my business life, Fear has to sit in the backseat. Actually, if my business is one of those white Ford Econoline vans that seats fourteen people, Fear sits way in the back and is forced to face out the back window. He doesn't get to look forward, talk to anyone else in the van, and he damn sure doesn't get any of the delicious homemade vegan chocolate chip cookies we're snacking on. As time has gone on and as I've put more projects out into the world, my white Ford Econoline has stretched longer and longer. With all of my business ideas filling the seats, Fear is pushed farther and farther back, and his space in the back is now even smaller with even less room to move than before.

Your metaphorical business automobile might be a Smart Car right now. It might feel like Fear is in the front with you, all up in your business. Or, worse, it might feel like Fear is the driver, and you're on the roof clutching for dear life. That's okay (metaphorically of course, if you're currently clutching the roof of a car, please put this book down and call for help).

Whenever Fear tries to take the wheel in your business, and especially when Fear tries to stop you from sticking your neck out and making an ask, simply consider this question: What's the worst thing that could happen?

Cliché, I know, but try it. Be 100 percent honest with yourself in your answer. Do you *truly* believe that launching the website for the business idea you have will leave you in the gutter, penniless, devoid of friends and family? Or is that just Fear driving your Smart Car again?

The worst outcome you can think of is never the outcome that actually happens. Even the most über successful of people in this world, who are also often those most willing to take risks, never end up in extreme dire situations because they took a risk with their businesses. The important next step after asking "What's the worst that could happen?" is to . . . you guessed it . . . test that assumption! Try having a conversation with Fear that goes something like this:

Fear: Jason, if you do this crazy WatchMeWrite idea for this book, people are going to laugh at your terrible writing, they are going to unsubscribe from your emails, they are going to ask for their money back on everything they've ever bought from you, and not a single person (not even your mom!) will buy your book.

Me: Okay Fear, I've heard you. I've let you have your moment to go through my worst-case scenario. Now, can we agree to just try this and see what happens?

Fear: I guess, but I still think you might end up naked in front of ten thousand people if you do this.

Me: That's a little far-fetched, don't you think?

Fear: Only for someone like you, I still think you're going to fail, but fine, let's see what happens.

Me: Byeeeeeeee.

Silly? Yes. But if you don't confront Fear and challenge what it's telling you by testing your assumptions, your business Econoline will never leave the parking lot.

WHEN YOU ASK AND THEY SAY NO

So what happens when you put yourself out there and someone says no? Then what? Is there any way to avoid it feeling completely soul-crushing? Here are a couple of things to remember that help with the potential sting of rejections.

PEOPLE AREN'T SAYING "NO" BECAUSE YOU'RE A BAD PERSON

Early on, I took a "no" to mean I was doing something wrong and that I should feel bad about it. When you hear no, the immediate reaction is to wonder what YOU did wrong. Is it that you're not good enough? That you didn't ask in the right way? That you should have tried harder? The questions don't end. But the more you ask, the more you start to realize those noes you're hearing very often have little or nothing to do with you.

Here are a few different examples of why people say "no" that have nothing to do with you as a person:

- **The timing is wrong**—I see this all the time. In fact, I tend to see it every year during the months of June, July, August, and December. Those are the worst months, historically, for me, and the onslaught of "noes." People are busy with other things. They're trying to take time off. Or, it's the end of the year and they can't be bothered. I do not control the timing and schedules of other people; therefore, I am not a bad person.

- **It isn't in the budget**—You simply can't do anything about other people's budgets. You can't. If I could, I would invent a magic wand that increases budgets. Then, I would wave this wand more than Harry Potter does in all 16,712 Harry Potter books.

- **It doesn't fit with their marketing plan**—Well, guess what? You and I didn't create their marketing plan! Moving on.

- **They've tried this type of thing before and had a bad experience**—I don't get this one as often with my weird ideas, but I do get it with products I sell that have been similar to other products out there. We can't change a person's experience with another product. We can give them an opportunity to change their mind, but that's for another chapter of this book.

- **They don't see the value**—This is the only example on this list that gets a bit tricky. It's either a problem with how you and I are explaining our project and the value proposition behind it, or, the person we're trying to get a "yes" from just doesn't get it. I imagine you know I've dealt with this a time or two.

I could go on and on with more examples. The point is: You need to remove yourself, and the feeling of being personally attacked, when someone says "no" to you.

HEARING "NO" IS JUST ANOTHER OPPORTUNITY TO HEAR "YES"

We learn way more from our failures than we do our successes. When someone says no, you have to see it as one more opportunity to hone your ask, your skill, your offer, etc. And then you try something different the next time. Don't forget the lesson from Chapter 4: Run toward rejection. Use it as fuel and motivation to get to your yes.

I want you to imagine the number of times I've been said "no" to for my ideas. Whether it was trying to convince companies to buy my T-shirt advertising space, to place a bid to own my last name, to sponsor a page in my first book, or to buy one of the twenty plus products I've released in the past few years.

Do you have your number?

If your number was under a hundred, you have a lot of faith in me and I love you for that, but oh no, I'm so sorry, you were way off. If your number was lower than five thousand, you would also be wrong.

I'm sure the actual number of times I've been told "no" when asking someone to pay me money for something (since 2008) is higher than five thousand. Here's how I can confidently say that:

- I wrote at least one thousand personal tweets to people asking for them to buy sponsorship days with IWearYourShirt.

- I sent at least five hundred emails in 2009 to companies to sponsor IWearYourShirt.

- I wrote more than twenty-five hundred emails to people I'd worked with previously (or had talked to previously) to sponsor my book.

- I had a spreadsheet of two hundred and fifty companies I pitched to bid on my last name.

- I've sent over fifty emails to my various email lists (that range in size from two thousand to twenty-five thousand people) asking them to buy my products.

Boy oh boy, have I racked up the "noes." But, in the game of asking, you realize it's all a numbers game. Only a small percentage of people you actually ask will say yes, which means with every ask—even if the response is a no—you're getting close to that inevitable YES reply that you're hoping for.

OWNING YOUR ASKING WEIRD

Remember my SponsorMyBook project I told you about? The project where I got 204 companies to sponsor little 140 character messages on the pages of my self-published book, *Creativity for Sale?* One of those available sponsor spots for a company was logo space on the front cover of the book (the cover sponsor). When I was thinking of companies that would be a good fit, the folks at Gumroad.com came to mind. Gumroad is a simple online software application that helps you sell digital products. I thought they'd be the perfect fit for the cover sponsor of my book (a $20,000 ask). Through some Internet sleuthing, I found a guy on Twitter who was doing marketing for Gumroad.

I sent my pitch email about my $20,000 sponsorship request (ballsy, yes) and was happy to get a quick reply from the guy—until I saw it was a big fat no. For some odd reason, I wasn't ready to accept defeat in that moment. I fired back an email that went something like this:

"Hey <person>! Thanks for the quick reply. I totally understand this type of sponsorship isn't a good fit for everyone. That being said, is there any chance you can think of anyone off the top of your head that might be a good fit? If you have an email address or have the time to make a super-quick intro, I would greatly appreciate it!"

I had no clue if that message would actually get a worthwhile response and any meaningful introductions. But hey, as the not-so-old-adage-you-just-learned goes, you don't get what you don't ask for!

The email response that followed was exactly what I'd hoped for. The guy had two companies he thought would be interested and he was willing to make a short email intro for me. BOOMSHAKALAKA! Needless to say, I was stoked. I didn't know if these email intros would turn into anything, but for the first time in my life, I had taken a "no" email and turned it into a potential "yes."

That email response led to two introductions, one of which was the CEO of a company called Treehouse, an online education platform. I'd actually met the CEO, Ryan Carson, at a Future of Web Apps (FOWA!) conference many years prior. While the introduction was great, I still had to put in the work to convince Ryan that Treehouse would be a good fit for the $20,000 sponsorship I was asking for.

See, you may think a warm introduction will do the work for you, but that's just the beginning. I had to hunker down and prove to Treehouse that this was a great opportunity for them. The more I looked into all the different things they teach creative entrepreneurs on Treehouse, the more I knew they'd be the absolute perfect fit to sponsor the cover of my book.

The response from the warm introduction was a great start. Ryan was interested in the sponsorship opportunity for Treehouse. But he wanted to know a bunch more. We exchanged a few emails back and forth, and while Ryan wasn't saying "no," he also wasn't writing checks. I knew I needed to up the ante. I started thinking to myself: *This is a creative sponsorship for a creative company.* Just typing words in an email isn't going to land the deal. What could I do that would be *weird* and really show Ryan this was worth it for Treehouse?

I could mock up a cover of a book and mail it to him, I thought. While that seemed interesting, it felt like it would take too long and wouldn't have a huge impact.

I could create a specific landing page on the SponsorMyBook website that shared why this was a good fit. After about thirty minutes into working on that, it felt as un-impactful as the emails I'd already been sending.

Then I had the thought to create a short video. I'd been making videos for years and it was something I could quickly and easily do. Plus, if it was unique, it would feel like I put a lot of time and creative energy into it.

I jotted down a few ideas for the video, but the one that stood out was to hand-draw my explanation of the sponsorship, the book, and how Treehouse could fit in nicely. I opened up a text-editing app on my laptop and typed out a very loose script for the video (one I'd record as a voiceover to the drawings). Then, I grabbed a pen and some printer paper and illustrated my little story.

Remember our friend Fear? Well, he started to climb from the back of the van toward the front seat, saying things like:

- "Jason, you're not a full-time illustrator, what makes you think your mediocre drawing skills will work?"

- "You've never done a video like this, it's going to suck!"

- "When you finish this video, Ryan and his entire team are going to laugh at you, share this horrible video with the world, and then you'll end up pants-less in front of a crowd of ten thousand people!"

As you know, I heard Fear out for a moment but quickly pushed him to the back of the van and got to work. Drawing. Typing. Filming. Redrawing. Cutting out my drawings with scissors that barely fit in my giant hands. Then editing. Refilming. And so on. About forty-eight hours later I had a finished video.

I uploaded the video, copied the URL. Wrote a quick email to Ryan saying something cryptic like, "I know we've exchanged a few emails about this sponsorship, I hope this helps sway you . . . <youtube link>." Then I hit send. I owned my weird with this ask.

Then I waited.

And waited.

And waited some more.

A few hours later, I received a reply from Ryan, "Jason, we loved the video! We're in. I'm attaching a colleague to this email who will work with you going forward. Excited to sponsor your book!"

WAHOO! Jubilation! Excitement! Adjectives! My gamble had paid off. Owning my weird and going with an out-of-the-box idea worked. And not just my gamble to make a video, but my gamble to ask a person who said "no" to me to shift to saying "yes."

Now for some honesty because that's how I roll: that's been my biggest victory in turning a "no" into a "yes." Sure, I've had a handful of other victories over the years. However, I've had my fair share of additional "nos" as well. And the pile of additional "nos" is exponentially taller than the pile of converted "nos to yeses." But I just keep trying.

Why?

I want what's on the other side of asking more than I fear the rejection that comes from making an ask. **I want to succeed more than I'm afraid to fail.**

I'm willing to put myself out on the line because I know that's what it takes to have incredible things happen in life.

What I want you to remember is that you have so much more to gain from making an ask than you have to lose. Making an ask of any kind is hard enough, but doing it while also trying to own your weird is even harder. The sooner you can learn to muster up the courage to put yourself out there (and the sooner you can learn to cope with rejection), the more asking you can do and the more opportunities you can create for yourself.

Chapter 16: "Own it!" recap and to-do item

- I know deep down in my gut that you have something you've been meaning to ask someone for. I understand you're afraid of the possible rejection, but trust me when I say that you won't end up covered in scorpions, naked, and broadcasted to the entire world live for everyone to point and laugh (what, that's not your go-to worst-case scenario?). How can you own your weird a bit and make your ask more compelling or unique? Don't drag your feet, just make your ask different and then send it out!

CHAPTER 17

Balance Optimism with Realism

Any kind of pioneer in any field has the very tough task of walking the thin line between optimism and realism. Sometimes owning your weird requires you to believe in a vision that no one else can see, which often requires optimism. You have faith that in your journey to carve out your own path, things will turn out fine. But, as essential as that belief and optimism is, we can't just pretend that there aren't real forces in the world that play a role in your decision-making—forces like money and family and supporting your lifestyle. That's where the balancing act comes in.

PUT FOOD ON YOUR TABLE FIRST

We've all heard of the notion of the "starving artist," right? Well, I believe we've moved into the era of the "starving entrepreneur," now that the Internet tells all.

Truthfully, the "starving entrepreneur" has always existed, but I see it running rampant through the streets these days like never before. There seems to be these two extreme pictures being painted. You either LOVE what you do (likely meaning you've created your own job and started your own business) OR you HATE your job. Starting a business is touted as the ultimate freedom and "regular jobs" are villainized. But there is SO much room for nuance in the middle.

I see people quitting their jobs to start their own businesses, and while I certainly can respect the courage it takes to make that kind of leap, unfortunately sometimes I see it lead to a different kind of crippling stress. By putting all the financial pressure on whatever it is you love to do, you run the risk of strangling your creativity.

Do you know how much easier it is to create when you're in a place of less pressure and stress? When what you're creating doesn't dictate whether you're going to be able to put a meal on your table or not, your creativity isn't hindered by a literal fear of survival.

I'm all for taking risks. In fact, some people might even say it's how I've made my career as an entrepreneur (right next to owning my weird). But here's the thing that most people don't see with any "risk" I take . . . It's *calculated*.

- How much time will this project take to build?

- Do I have time to build this project?

- How much time will this project take on an ongoing basis?

- Do I have time for that?

- How much money will this project cost to make?

- Do I have this amount of money to invest?

- How much money can this project make me?

- Is that amount worth the juice-squeezing?

- How will this project affect my life if it fails miserably into a burning inferno, wrapped in molten lava, shot off into space never to be seen again?

- What is my absolute worst-case scenario?

- What is my best-case scenario?

There hasn't been a single project I've taken on, launched, or put out into the world that had to be wildly financially successful to put food on my table. Sure, my projects have to make me money, but I'm always hedging my bets. I'm preparing for success *and* failure.

Let's hop in the Jason Zook Time Machine. (Keep your legs and arms inside the carpet at all times! Aladdin reference, anyone?) Back in 2007 when I decided I was going to leave the 9-to-5 world to start a design agency with a friend (this is pre-IWearYourShirt), I didn't just quit my job and dive headfirst into the entrepreneurial deep end. I did everything in my power to prepare for that design agency to be successful (and I had a backup plan in case I failed).

Since this was my first time dipping my toes in the entrepreneurial pool, I was way more cautious than I am today. I told myself I needed six months to build up the business on the side, save money from my paychecks, and, most important, muster up the courage to leave the safety net of a normal job and consistent income.

For those six months, I put in three to five hours per night building my design agency. I would email people and ask them if they needed design work (or if they knew anyone who needed design work). I would have conversations with my co-founder (of a company of two) regarding ways we could get our work noticed by other people. We even built our first little web application that showed off our skills to attract design clients. We did a lot of work in those six months, but I also squirreled chunks of money away like they were acorns and I was headed for a long, bitter winter. Slowly, we added paying clients to our little design business, but I still wanted to make sure I had a backup plan (even if that backup plan meant I may have to completely change my lifestyle).

Here are a few of the things I did to make sure I always had a plan in place to have food on my table:

1. I stayed at my 9-to-5 job and saved as much money as I could (limiting my spending for six months). Eventually, I had six months of basic living expenses in my savings account.

2. I built a "worst-case scenario plan." This consisted of telling myself that selling my car, moving in with my family, and eating ramen noodles would be okay for awhile. Sure, it would suck royally, but it would only be temporary.

3. I made sure to give myself permission to crawl back to my 9-to-5 job, or to get another one, if my savings ran out and my design agency failed.

I see lots of entrepreneurs, solopreneurs, and creative people wanting to dive into the deep end of starting their own thing without any semblance of a backup plan. Sure, that method of thinking works for about fourteen entrepreneurs in our society (most of which have had movies made about them that likely don't tell the whole story), but it's simply not a smart decision for the rest of us.

Putting food on your table first gives you the space to not have to worry or be stressed out. It's not the sexy backstory you want to tell your kids: "And then Mom saved up for six months so she'd have a nice, warm, comfortable blanket of savings to fall back on, just in case." Call me overly practical, but I don't think the entrepreneurial-hustle-porn we all get shown is in any way good for us. I do believe in taking risks—lots of them, in fact. But more specifically, I believe in taking calculated risks that won't ever take a (delicious) plant-based meal off my table.

It may take you six months, or it may take you less or more. That's not a standard amount of time that everyone has to follow, it was just my randomly chosen length of time from back in 2007 when I was planning to step out on my own. You get to decide the amount of time you think is best for you while you build your game plan.

Even with a six-month buffer, I still felt the pressure when I left my cushy 9-to-5 job and cannonballed my way into the deep end of the pool. This is normal. With any risk you take, there will always be pressure to not belly flop. But if you build up a buffer for yourself, that pressure won't be crippling.

You may need to change your lifestyle for a while. You may need to cut way back on spending. You may need to sell your car and start riding a bike. You may need to cancel all your Netflix/Hulu/HBO subscriptions so you can save every penny. Only you know your own tolerance for risk. What I'm trying to posit to you is that it's foolish to dive in without a plan and without some sort of buffer in place. You probably didn't expect to read this from the guy who's started businesses built on paid T-shirt wearing, last name pimping, future selling, etc. But again, all of those crazy ideas have had backup plans.

SET REALISTIC EXPECTATIONS

Balancing optimism and realism relates especially to business when it comes to setting expectations for your business or your project. Remember when I told you about my first online course and how I was trying to make $100,000 with it? My expectations were through the roof! The worst part? I had a sizable audience, so this blind optimism felt like it was actually based in reality. It seemed possible. In fact, I convinced myself over and over again that it would definitely happen—and more specifically, that it *had* to happen—because I wasn't starting from scratch. (If you don't remember, I ended up making $5,200 at the launch of the course, which was about $94,800 short of my goal. Whoops.)

Here's how I've learned from my past mistakes and developed a system of setting expectations that leave room for optimism AND realism.

LOW GOALS AND HIGH GOALS FOR PROJECTS

With every project I begin, I do a super-simple exercise (after I've already decided the juice is worth the squeeze, I can afford the time/money the project will take, and that I'm ready for the worst- or best-case scenarios): I establish low and high financial goals. The low goal serves as my realism weight and I tend to set this based on my own personal experience and real "data." The high goal serves as my optimism weight and I allow myself to set this based on nothing more than my belief in myself and my idea. Using these two different goals, I'm able to protect myself from going way offtrack with wild projection and being totally disappointed, while also putting positive thoughts into my abilities and the possibilities that could come from doing things differently.

Let's look at a couple of specific examples.

IWEARYOURSHIRT

This was an insane business idea. Ask people around the world to pay me, a virtual nobody (literally and figuratively), to wear their shirt and promote their company on burgeoning social media sites. But make no mistake, I started IWearYourShirt with a backup plan. I was still working at my design agency and getting paid a monthly salary to keep food on the ol' plate. During the first few weeks of launching IWearYourShirt in late 2008, things were looking grim. Not only did I know the business wouldn't make real money (read, more than a couple of hundred dollars) until I sold over one-third of the calendar spots, but I also didn't know if I could keep up the daily pace I had set for myself. Behind the scenes I established a low goal and a high goal:

- **Low goal: Do everything in my power from October 1, 2008, to December 31, 2008, to promote and sell IWearYourShirt calendar spots.** Whatever spots I sold, I would follow through on. If I didn't sell more than one-third of the calendar by December 31, 2008, I would do the work I'd promised for the folks who purchased and just let the project do whatever it could organically do. If I didn't sell more than the first month, I would refund all purchases, put my tail between my legs, and retreat into my entrepreneurial dog house (still having my design agency to fall back on) and that would be fine.

- **High goal: SELL ALL THE THINGS!** By all the things I mean all 365 calendar spots available for 2009. Nothing beyond that. I promised myself not to get caught up in the dreams and grand ideas of what IWearYourShirt could become. If all 365 spots sold, I'd think about moving to IWearYourShirt full-time and leave the design agency.

- **Result: I landed somewhere in the middle.** By December 31, 2008, I sold just under 50 percent of the calendar spots. Because I set my low goal fairly low, I was stoked. (Literally my baseline was just to have the courage to put the crazy idea out there and promote it.) And, even more awesome, my high goal was actually within striking distance. I could see the potential of hitting the high goal, something that gave me momentum and motivation.

BUYMYLASTNAME

If wearing sponsored T-shirts was insane, then donning a sponsored last name for a year would equate to Tesla's "Ludicrous Mode"! In truth, I had no idea if people would get this concept. Having a brand as a last name for a year and just living my life? Even I was a little skeptical, but I also believed there was something worth pursuing, so I did. (Plus, a divorce in my family had left me with a last name I no longer wanted, and what's a guy to do when he doesn't have a last name he loves? Sell it, obviously!)

- **Low goal: During the thirty-day auction for my last name, my low goal was to hit $5,000.** If I could hit $5,000, that would be enough money for me to live on for two months. At the time (2012), my IWearYourShirt business was fizzling out and I needed to start thinking about my next move (to put food on my table!).

- **High goal: Have the auction reach $100,000.** That was my pipe dream. But, and this goes for all my high goals, I wouldn't judge the success of the project on the high goal. This was just to establish a fun motivating thought in my mind. High goals can honestly be very distracting when you don't take the time to determine a solid number you're reaching for.

- **Result: I nearly had my socks blown right off my feet.** In the first twenty-four hours after launching the website, the bidding had gone from $0 to $33,333. See ya later, low goal! You've been shattered! Truthfully, the shattering of that low goal did have me chomping at the bit to try to reach my high goal of $100,000. However, whenever I'd be venturing down the mental path of dreaming about hitting my high goal, I would remind myself that my low goal had been demolished (and that was an awesome thing). This helped keep my ever-growing expectations in check.

SPONSORMYBOOK

I wanted to challenge the notion that first-time authors couldn't make money with a book. I also wanted to do it without the help of a book agent or book publisher. (There I go again, owning my weird.) I knew I had experience selling sponsorships, but this idea was something that hadn't been done before (imagine that). To get hundreds of companies to pay to have their names in a book that didn't yet exist, by an author who'd never written anything before, was going to be a challenge.

- **Low goal: Get two hundred companies to sponsor pages in the book.** Wait, that doesn't seem like a low goal, that's how many sponsors were available (minus the cover sponsors)! My "ace in the hole" was that I would do everything in my power to sell the sponsorships by February 1, 2014 (I started five months prior). If I got close to February 1 and still had sponsor spots available, I'd just start giving them away to charitable organizations for free. Based on my experience working with over sixteen hundred businesses during my IWearYourShirt days, this low-high goal still felt very realistic.

- **High goal: Get two hundred paying sponsors, every page of the book, plus four cover sponsors (front cover, back cover, and two inside flaps).** If every sponsor spot was sold at face value—a face value I made up—the total amount of money the project would make was $158,000.

- **Result: I ended selling all 204 sponsorships!** High goal met! (Kind of.) As I just said, I was supposed to make $158,000 if all the sponsorships sold at the face value I set. But, haggling ensued. Partially, it happened because I just wanted to sell the damn sponsorships already and I realized the face value pricing I'd set was completely arbitrary. I sent many an email back to interested sponsors with "just name a fair price, and let's make it happen!" I ended up netting $75,000 for the project and couldn't have been happier. Low goal attained. High goal achieved. Win-win!

BUYMYFUTURE

We've gone from Ludicrous Mode . . . to . . . downright out-of-this-galaxy mode. Who sells their future? Who lets people stop paying them money forever? This guy! That's who. In the fall of 2015 when I started BuyMyFuture, I had income from multiple revenue sources. As far as food on my table goes, I didn't have money for a Thanksgiving dinner plate every night, but I had built a bit more of a buffer than I'd ever had (plus, I had the opportunity to make money by doing promotions and other things with those businesses). It had taken me ten years, but I was finally in a more secure place, and making any money from BuyMyFuture was just the (vegan) gravy on my mashed potatoes.

- **Low goal: Get 10 people to buy (at $1,000 per sale).** Small. Simple. Achievable. If my other ideas felt hard to sell, this one felt nearly impossible (which is often the case when you really apply the Own Your Weird mindset to a business idea). It was even far out there for *me*, and that's saying something.

- **High goal: 1,000 buyers (that would total $1,000,000).** I'd never done a $1,000,000 product launch. Heck, who am I kidding, I'd never done a $100,000 launch. But this was the wildly high goal that came to my mind that I wanted to let myself entertain.

- **Result: 178 purchases and a total of $178,000.** I put more effort into selling BuyMyFuture than anything I'd ever sold before. So much so, that before the project launched publicly, I had already met my low goal. I did a ton of work leading up to the start of BuyMyFuture (including a daily blog, written for sixty days straight), but kept mystery around the actual project. Part of that work leading up to the launch was hopping on Skype calls with forty-nine people, one by one. These previous customers of mine learned about the idea and gave me feedback on it (notice that feedback came from people who'd already paid me money in the past!). Ten of them begged me to be able to purchase early (oh, you're begging to give me $1,000? That's a high goal in itself!). My low goal was easily met, and a funny thing happened with my high goal. No, I didn't make $1,000,000 with 1,000 sales, but I did realize I actually didn't want to meet my high goal. Managing

1,000 customers sounded like a nightmare! I was perfectly happy to land 178 customers for the first BuyMyFuture launch.

The great thing about playing the low goal/high goal game is that you set your own expectations AND you get them out of your head. For me, the high goal is always a huge reach. It's usually something I'm not sure I could get to (or in some cases, it would be mind-blowing if I got to it), so if I get anywhere close to it, it's a huge moral victory.

Meeting and exceeding your low goals are how you measure your success. Acknowledging your high goals and not focusing too heavily on them are how you stay sane.

Because I set these two types of goals with every single project I work on, I'm not left wondering about the success of each project. Better yet, I always start a project knowing how the outcomes will affect my life and my reflection on that project.

Managing your own expectations is the best thing you can do when starting any new project or business to make sure the outcome stays productive. You can't force the hand of your customers. You can't predict the behavior of the people who have the wallets/purses you're going after. But you can quiet the voices in your head by getting clear with what you expect to happen and what you want to happen.

This advice doesn't just have to apply to business, either. Whenever you're owning your weird, you're going out on a limb and the outcome is often wildly unknown. Whether you're changing your diet or moving somewhere or making a change of any kind in your life to reflect your true self better, you'll need to balance optimism with realism. Believe in what you're doing and all the amazing possibilities that could come from your big change, and then react to the practical realism of what you see in front of you.

Chapter 17: "Own it!" recap and to-do item

• Are you about to start a new business, launch a new product, or embark on a personal change of some sort that you can measure? Let's set a LOW and HIGH goal so you can "own it" with your expectations. Write these two numbers down and focus only on accomplishing your low goal. Remember, your high goal is just to get it out of your head so it doesn't consume you. When you hit your low goal, you know what to do right? "I OWWWWWWNED IT!" (again, best yelled in a public place).

CHAPTER 18

Focus on Completion, Not Perfection

A few years ago when someone subscribed to my weekly email newsletter (*The Action Army*), I used to ask one simple question: what's the thing you're struggling with the most right now? The replies I saw most often were

- I want to start my own business, but I don't have the *perfect* idea yet.

- I'm working on launching my business, but I haven't *perfected* the product/service yet.

- I feel paralyzed by the amount of information I read and wish I had the *perfect* step-by-step process to do XYZ.

There's one word I kept seeing over and over again: perfect. If you're ever going to embrace your uniqueness and learn what your strengths are, you have to experiment (a lot) and use pattern recognition to look back at your work and learn from it. But that means you have to get out there and do stuff. A lot of stuff.

The problem, though, is that so many people are afraid of doing anything at all because of that pesky little thing called perfection. Perfection is a giant roadblock that can stop you from ever starting and that can stop you from ever *finishing*.

WHY WE AIM FOR PERFECTION

We take fourteen versions of a selfie to make sure we look the best. We write and rewrite status updates and messages to each other trying to sound witty or smart. We buy clothes that accentuate our best features. We want to optimize everything and put forth the glossiest, most flawless version of ourselves possible.

And we do the same thing with our ideas.

Why? Because we're *afraid*. Afraid that someone will think less of us. That they'll judge us for being imperfect, or that they'll judge our weird ideas and reject us for them. We disguise this fear by turning it into perfection, which ultimately leads to procrastination and an inability to just complete whatever it is we set out to do.

You know what I'm talking about. The brand or website you've been working on for a year but won't publish because it's not "perfect." The business you won't start because you don't have the perfect name or perfect team or perfect process for it yet.

The sooner you accept that perfection is just fear, the sooner you can get the courage to overcome it and start actually taking action (read: putting your ideas out into the world).

Striving for perfection is the ultimate reliance on assumptions. "This isn't good enough yet." "It's not ready." "I'm not ready." The key, as we've already discussed together in this book, is in actually testing these assumptions. You have to train your brain to focus on completion rather than perfection. Focusing on completion will ensure that you're actually out there in the field gathering data and getting real feedback, not just the feedback you're imagining in your head.

PERFECTION PREVENTS
YOU FROM STARTING

This is one of those lessons you can hear a million times, but won't believe until you have the experience yourself.

When it comes to starting a new project, new business, or putting a new idea out into the world, you are NEVER ready. There's no such thing as a starting finish line. There's just a starting line. And with every starting line I've ever seen in business, the accompanying finish line is hidden around future curves, hills, mountains, meteor showers, and the eventual fall off the edge of the track (only to hang on by one fingertip, Super Mario 64–style.)

Here's the problem with new ideas and new things: they're *new*. They're not proven. They don't exist. You have to navigate all the murky waters of figuring out what starting looks like. You have to get over the notion that you will have it all figured out and perfect right out of the gate.

This instinct—to stop yourself before you even start—comes from a few places. First, you don't want to waste your first impression. I get that. In business especially, first impressions do count. But there's a lot of room between something that's not good enough to be seen and something that's not perfect. There's a whole spectrum in between those two extremes. You have to get honest with yourself about whether something isn't ready because it won't make a good first impression, or if you're actually the one who isn't ready—ready to face your fears.

Second, if you never start, you never fail. I see this one a lot. If you don't put yourself out there, you can't get rejected, right? But hopefully by now I've convinced you that the risk is unavoidable. Not only is it unavoidable, it's well worth experiencing in exchange for what you get, which is the happiness of doing your own thing and doing it your own weird way.

Third, you're an optimizer. This is what Caroline calls someone who wants to maximize every possible decision and deeply fears the regret of making a less-than-perfect decision. This is the person that can't decide on a business name because they're terrified of needing to change it years down the road for any number of random scenarios. If this is you, remember that optimizing is a game that's played in your head, not real life. Owning your weird is about testing your assumptions.

You have to take action and learn by doing. It may be scary to risk regret by starting, but at least by making some kind of decision you're moving forward rather than staying still.

Fourth, if you haven't created many things before, it feels like the weight of the world rests in just that one thing. This is the hardest thing to explain to someone who doesn't have a lot of experience owning their weird or making things. If you never put your ideas or work out there, the pressure to have that one thing be perfect feels crushing. It isn't until you have those multiple chances at bat (through consistency) that you realize there's less pressure for that one thing to be perfect because tomorrow there's another chance to make something new or to improve (or, make it weirder!).

PERFECTION PREVENTS
YOU FROM FINISHING

Let's say you manage to get over that first initial perfection roadblock and you do get started with an idea. You probably think you've bested the perfection boss and it's smooth sailing from there on out. Wrong. I guarantee you that the closer you get to the finish line (whatever that line is), the more perfection will start rearing its ugly head again, preventing you from finishing.

But, if you can retrain your brain to focus less on perfection and more on *completion*, you're sure to accomplish so much more. Don't worry about finishing a task in the perfect way, worry about finishing the task. Period.

By focusing on completion, things will actually get done. Right or wrong doesn't matter. What matters is that you are constantly moving yourself and your business forward.

I've fallen into the trap of aiming for perfection many times. Back in 2008 when I was looking to launch IWearYourShirt, I had placed a daunting task ahead of myself: filming and editing a video every single day with zero filming experience. (This was WAY before daily vlogs were the norm on YouTube.) When I had committed to this path, I didn't even own a video camera or editing software. Scary, right? But what was even scarier were the thoughts that I let run rampant through my head. *This first video has to be perfect or else people will know I don't have any experience.*

At every stage in the process of filming my first video, I put an immense amount of pressure on myself to have the perfect lighting, audio, angle, and composition. The editing, I assumed, would have to be perfect, too. But I didn't even get to that point because I gave up shortly after I started. The pressure to reach perfection was too much.

Then a new thought occurred to me: *Holy crap, I'm committing to making 365 daily videos. How the hell am I going to get a perfect video done every day!?* Well, the short answer is: I'm not.

That's when I made the decision that I would **focus on completion and not perfection.** Just get each day's video done, I told myself. That was the goal. If it sucked, well there would just be a new video posted the next day and that would be my chance to get just a little bit better.

From that moment forward, I tried to not worry about the perfect anything. If I felt something was really wrong, I'd just film a second take or two. If I didn't love how I edited a text overlay on the video, I said I'd do a better job on the next one. Slowly but surely, I got better at making videos. I am 100 percent aware that my early videos are terrible. But the important part is they got made. I completed them. And I learned. Had I not published the not-so-good stuff, I wouldn't have been able to get to the actually pretty-good stuff. Those early videos helped move my business forward, one step at a time.

Let this be a constant reminder for all of us: done is better than perfect.

PERFECT DOES NOT EXIST

Let me remind you of those struggles I used to hear from subscribers of my email list: I want to start my own business, but I don't have the *perfect* idea yet. I'm working on launching my business, but I haven't *perfected* the product/service yet. I feel paralyzed by the amount of information I read and wish I had the *perfect* step-by-step process to do XYZ. The reply I often want to send back to those people is just one sentence long, all caps, and it says: PERFECT DOES NOT EXIST! (But, I'm not that shouty so I restrain myself.) Let's go through these, though, so we can get to the truth of each one.

COMING UP WITH "THE PERFECT IDEA"

I hate to be the bearer of bad news, but there is no such thing as a perfect idea. There are good ideas. There are bad ideas. There are fun ideas. There are stupid ideas. But no idea is ever perfect by itself.

Once you get that idea of perfection out of your head you can start looking at your ideas from a different angle. For me, I look for ideas I can't get out of my head. Maybe the "perfect" idea is just the one you can't get out of your head. It's the one that's nagging at you, following you around, and that means you'll put forth the most effort to bring it to life. Mark Cuban has said "Don't follow your passions, follow your effort." Where you apply your time is where you will succeed, and that's the secret to the perfect idea—the one you'll put time and effort into.

Here's how that works for me on a practical level:

- Step 1—When I have an idea, I write a couple of bullet points about it in a journal. I do this as soon as the idea comes to me.

- Step 2—I put the journal (and idea) away for a week. I don't write anything else about it and I don't spend any time building a prototype version of it. I just let the idea sit.

- Step 3—If I can't stop thinking about the idea after a week I take the next steps to pursue it. If I've forgotten about the idea or it's no longer nagging at me, I move on.

Instead of looking for a perfect idea, look for something you simply can't stop thinking about. Trust your gut and listen for things that feel right. When an idea or a thought continues to nag at you over and over again, it's important to listen to your instincts. It can be easy to let yourself get caught up in what other people are doing, but oftentimes what other people are doing is not the thing we should be doing (or the Own Your Weird way we should be doing it).

Listening to your gut is also the best way to make decisions based on your values and beliefs. There's a deeper part of you that knows what you really want, and paying attention to that will help you pursue the path that isn't perfect, but is right for you. Listening to your instincts can't guarantee that your idea will work, but at least you'll be making the choices based on what really matters deep down.

BUILDING "THE PERFECT BUSINESS"

You will never have a perfect business. There will always be some issue, problem, or *holy-shit-everything-is-going-wrong moment* that you'll have to overcome. It happens to us all. Accept this and focus on the things you *can* control: creating a quality product, having amazing customer service, focusing on making your customers more awesome, and embracing your weirdness in your business so it stands out. Businesses have so many moving parts to them that you're better off getting started, making sure all the plates are in the air and spinning, and then you can go back through and tweak the balance on all of them once you have *real* experience to back your decisions.

CREATING "THE PERFECT PROCESS"

One of the destructive ways that perfectionism poisons our minds is through the widespread illusion that success in business is simple. We see it in articles like the "sixteen tactics to insane profitability" or "what one simple thing brought in six figures in additional revenue" propaganda we read every single day on "reputable" news sources.

There are too many success stories without enough focus on the times of non-success. In psychology, they call this *survivorship bias*—a logical error where we focus on those who have "survived" some process and inadvertently overlook those who didn't (probably because every magazine cover and news story focuses only on the huge wins).

This bias can distort our reality, causing us to falsely believe that the successes of a group are due to some special property they have that we don't. This cycle continues because we, as consumers of content (a.k.a. readers of websites, books, et al.), keep clicking the stupid clickbait headlines, hoping to find some magic pill, spell, or potion to solve our persistent woes.

(Please contact me if you've clicked one of these articles or read one of these books, learned a tip or tactic, applied it to your business, and enjoyed all the riches and success you were promised. I won't hold my breath for any of those emails to show up in my inbox.)

The process is not simple. The journey is not clear. The perfect process does not exist. What does exist, however, is the process you create for yourself and that works specifically for you. This comes with time and is never truly perfect. Remember, the blueprint can't be discovered; it has to be created. By you, for you.

YOUR PATH TO SUCCESS
IS A TREASURE MAP

Speaking of discovering your own imperfect process, it's time we redraw in our minds what the journey to success looks like. Magazines, TV shows, movies, and websites love to glamorize how people "made it" and "became so insanely rich they turned into a pile of money and flew off in the wind." (I may have made up the second example there.) The way that news articles and three-minute clips on TV or interview segments on talk shows often portray these stories is in a conveniently straight line. You start at your little dot on a map. Then you travel across a single line and you're at the X. Success!

Wrong.

Success doesn't look like a straight line; it looks like a treasure map. You follow a dotted line that twists, turns, curves, hits all kinds of obstacles in your way, sends you on a couple of wild goose chases, and eventually you find the X—*maybe*. Sometimes you get shipwrecked. Sometimes you get stranded. Sometimes your only friend is a volleyball. No one can predict when you'll fall off the map (read: when you will have a mistake or failure), but it *will* happen. It happens to everyone at some point or another—even the "overnight successes" portrayed by the media.

If you accept the fact that success looks like a treasure map, you won't be concerned when one of those detours occurs. When you veer off path, when you hit roadblocks, you'll be able to see them for what they are: interesting turns on your treasure map to happiness. As long as you're moving forward, you'll still know you're headed in the right direction. Remember our little mantra from earlier in the book: opportunities, not obstacles.

GET OFF THE FERRIS WHEEL OF PERFECTION

By chasing the perfect anything, you're essentially riding a Ferris wheel. As soon as you think you've reached the end, a new set of "problems" arise and you continue going around in a never-ending circle.

Instead of going around and around, focus on creating and trusting the path you have forged for yourself. If you're wondering, it's the one you won't be able to see laid out perfectly in front of you.

There's no such thing as a fully lit path. You simply need to give your ideas a chance. Believe in whatever process you choose. Build a business and life for yourself that you actually enjoy. The path will become illuminated bit by bit, just as headlights will light the way down a winding road you've never driven before.

Riding on the Ferris wheel of perfection is exhausting. Take the energy you would spend trying to remove perceived flaws and instead apply it to making *things—imperfect* things. This will also put you in a much happier position long-term. Instead of trying to keep up some flawless facade, if you establish early on that imperfections are a part of your work, if you own your weird, you get to build an audience that accepts you for being yourself. This goes back to the strategy of authenticity and consistency. Perfection isn't authentic because no one is perfect.

People know I'm not the best writer because I tell them. If I send out an email with a mistake or a misspelling, my audience looks past it because they're not entirely that surprised. It's less important to them that I spell perfectly then it is that I include my signature humor, random tangents, and any other ways I embrace my weirdness. I shift the focus away from perfection and onto my uniqueness and personality.

When you're able to let go of perfection and face the fear of actually putting yourself out there, while owning your weird, that's when you'll be one step closer to the life and business you ultimately want.

Chapter 18: "Own it!" recap and to-do item

- I would wager all the crazy socks in my sock drawer (and there are a few, especially my awesome taco socks!) that perfection is holding you back in some way right now, whether it's hitting send on a sales email, publishing an article, uploading a video to YouTube, or simply starting your first business. You're stuck in perfectionism's evil grasp and it's time to free yourself. Say it with me right now: "Perfectionism, BE GONE!" Let it out. Let perfectionism go. Hit send. Hit publish. Hit upload. Move forward, imperfectly.

CHAPTER 19

Define the Terms
of Your Success

As the old adage goes, hard work pays off. But where that adage stops short is in explaining that the "payoff" may not be the success of the idea you set out to work on.

Hard work often leads you to new realizations about yourself. Hard work often shows you the things you really don't want to be doing in life. Hard work can lead you to your next idea, project, business, etc., and it can do all that without actually delivering the end result that you set out to accomplish.

Reading about the success of other people, even some of my successes in this book, can be intoxicating. You want to replicate the stories and successes of others. Unfortunately that's impossible. You'll never have the same set of circumstances or reach the same outcomes.

What you *can* do is get inspired by the stories you read from other people. You can take multiple ideas and ways other people have done things, and smash them together like a big ball of clay. Different ideas from different people make your ball of clay colorful and unique. Sure, at certain times your ball of clay may look ugly. It will be misshapen. It may not resemble a business or any version of what you deem successful in the beginning. But no sculptor started out with a finished piece of art. They started out with a big, ugly ball of clay. Time, effort, and looking at their ball of clay from weird angles is how they were able to turn it into a piece of art. The same thing can be said for whatever it is you're working on.

If there's one thing I hope this book has made abundantly clear, it is that "success" as the world seems to define it is actually one big fat empty promise. There is no one-size-fits-all definition for success. We think it's money, but all the money in the world can't compensate for waking up in a life that feels out of sync with who you are and what your values are. You get to decide what the terms of your success are. You get to say if it's spending time with family or sleeping in until 10:30 or traveling the world or having a business that gives back to those less fortunate. Whatever those values are that drive you, start formulating your own definition of success based on how much of those things you can live out on a daily basis.

THE LONG WAY IS THE SHORTCUT

The more time you spend looking for the fast track to success, the longer you'll delay actually becoming successful. But, the more you embrace what makes you unique, the better chance you'll have of your ideas standing out and being shared.

I get, like, steam shooting out of my ears like a cartoon character angry when people ask me "but Jason, what's the ONE thing I need to know about XYZ?"

There's never a "ONE thing" answer. If there were, don't you think everyone would be sharing it? Nothing in life is had by doing just one thing. Well, nothing in life worth having (and actually enjoying) is had by doing just one thing. There's a ton of available short-term success you can grab. But **short-term success won't make you happy in the long run.**

If you can reframe your thinking while reading or watching something based on the success of someone else from "what one thing is the key to their success?" to "what one thing can I add to my personalized collection of learning?" you'll put yourself on a more sustainable track to success.

I have to do this same thing on a regular basis. I'll get forwarded an article or stumble across some story of someone that's truly inspiring. I go digging for the ONE THING. Then I pinch myself and remember finding that one thing is an illusion. Instead, I should find my own takeaways—the ones that feel relevant and personal to me—and add them to my toolbox. I may not use this toolbox right now, or tomorrow, or even in the next few months. But by keeping those takeaways in my mind (or in a nicely organized Google Doc), I can refer back to them and let them help me at a later date when I need them.

The fast track is a dream that people like to sell because, well, let's be honest, it sells. But if you're ready to trade in the easy dream for the harder-but-truer reality, here's how you get off the fast track–to-success train for good: **You accept the fact that the long way is the shortcut**. (Thanks again for another version of this quote by Seth Godin, who obviously read this book, left a stunningly good five-star review on Amazon, and couldn't wait to tell all his friends about it.)

If you're constantly searching for the shortcuts, it's usually a good sign you're on the wrong path. Why? Because you're not in it for the *journey*. It means you're working on something that you don't actually want to put in the hard work to accomplish, which means you're in it for the end game and not because you love it. True authors don't write books because they want to become bestsellers (that's what sleazy marketers do). True authors write books because they have a message (even a weird one) they feel they have to share with the world, a message that can't be summed up in 140 characters (or 280), one blog post, one article, or even an eighteen-minute TED Talk.

Don't get me wrong, hard work doesn't mean you always have to do things the hard way. That's what your toolbox of takeaways is for. You get to leapfrog the mistakes and failures of other people. Just understand that it may take a hundred shortcuts (or a thousand or ten thousand) to finally accomplish that "overnight success" you crave so badly.

HOW DO YOU KNOW
WHEN YOU'VE "MADE IT"?

When I tell you that "I've made it" I imagine that you immediately conjure up thoughts of me swimming through a pool of money like Scrooge McDuck. You think of me driving my Ferrari down a California highway with my nonexistent hair blowing in the wind. But for me, saying "I've made it" has nothing to do with the material or monetary goals in life. It has everything to do with having enough, being okay with enough, having control over the decisions I make in my daily life or in my many businesses, and trying to own my weird, regardless of what anyone thinks. That is my blueprint for a happy and successful life. Now I hope you feel empowered to go out there and create yours.

Conclusion:

Question Everything

In this messy thing called life, it's really easy to count ourselves out before we give ourselves a chance. That can stem from an experience when we're young (say, if a teacher says you can't make a living as an artist) or it can come from people close to you who are afraid to challenge convention (and they project their fears on you). We're all capable of great ideas. We're all able to make and build things that have never been made and built before. But most often, it's our own assumptions and self-defeating thoughts that get in the way. Sometimes we can't even see that the box we imagine ourselves in was just created by other people like us.

I hope this book gives you permission to let go of your assumptions about what you're capable of. Your self-defeating thoughts are not warranted, and you should question every single one of them. Embrace your weirdness and bash into the walls of life a bit more! Break them down and build them back up according to what's important to you.

We don't get another shot at this thing called life. That doesn't mean you need to play it safe; that means you need to live to your fullest potential.

THERE'S NOTHING SPECIAL ABOUT TODAY

Did you know that? There's nothing special about this week. There's nothing special about this month, either.

It isn't the start of a new year (unless you're reading this on January 1, in which case, that's a crazy coincidence). It isn't the *perfect* time when the stars align just right. There's no magic in the air that's going to help you.

But you don't need any of that, anyway. You never did.

THIS can still be the exact moment you decide to make a change.

Today can be the day you start a new journey in life. A journey to start a business you've always wanted to start. A journey to move somewhere in the world you've always wanted to live. A journey to jump into (or out of) a relationship. A journey to build a better version of yourself.

Living an intentional life, where you embrace your uniqueness, where you own your weird, where you call the shots, doesn't happen because your decision coincides with the start of a new year, month, or week. It happens because you decide it happens.

You didn't get into your current circumstances overnight, and you won't get out of them overnight. Nothing worth having comes easily.

It's going to be hard.

It's going to take effort.

It's going to take sacrifices.

Hardly anything worth doing in life is going to happen by consuming more information (via social media, news, this book, etc.). You have ALL the right tools, all the knowledge, and all the time you ever need. You just need to be willing to take a chance.

You need to want the outcome more than you fear the reality.

There's nothing special about today, except today could be the day you change your life. And I hope it is.

Make today the day.

Own Your Weird!

Afterword

WatchMeWrite . . . Live

Writing a book was no easy feat. You may have read this book while on a journey to write your own book. Awesome! You may be thinking there's a book in you that you want to share with the world. Also awesome! You may not ever want to write a book in your life. Good for you and your sanity!

If you can believe it, I did something pretty . . . *weird* . . . when writing the book that's currently in your hands. I wrote the entire first draft live, for anyone (and everyone) to watch. I conjured up the idea while eating dinner with Caroline and scribbled it in a small journal I carry around with me often.

While waiting for our food to be delivered to our table, the idea that hit me was to let people see behind the scenes what it takes to write the first draft of a book. I knew I couldn't show the entire process live because most of it involves extremely boring hard work, but I thought I could share the first draft getting written.

Should I just write in a public Google Doc? Nah, that's boring and anyone could do that. Not weird enough.

Should I use something like Twitch? Eh, I'm not interested in using someone else's platform. Again, not weird enough.

Will anyone even care to watch me write? Who knows, but let's test that assumption! Also, "watch me write" is kind of a fun name.

I scribbled some initial weird thoughts about trying to make it fun for people to watch (i.e., gamification). I wanted each day's writing session to only be available for a short window of time. If you missed that day's live writing, you could donate a couple bucks to see the previous entry. I also thought that I could get sponsors to financially support the idea, since it was really unique and may be a perfect fit for their target audience of customers.

When we got home from dinner that night, I immediately sketched a wireframe for what I thought the "watch me write" website could look like when I was/wasn't writing live. I then logged into my Google Domains account and searched for a few domains. All the .com domains for any combination of words are typically taken by bridge-dwelling-domain-squatting-trolls. But, I'm okay with .co domains, and was happy to find that watchmewrite.co hadn't been squatted on (yay for another domain with "I" or "me" or "my" in it, haha!).

I started to make a list of features for WatchMeWrite and how I wanted people to be able to interact with my writing. I shared the initial idea with my buddy Paul Jarvis, who didn't hate it (haha, I think he actually said it was cool, but it's more fun to add a little drama here) and then shared with the folks in my BuyMyFuture community (who really liked it!). The initial feedback was great, but regardless of what other people thought about the idea, it was already consuming most of my waking thoughts. (Remember, this is my only criteria for the "perfect" idea.)

The next few days I spent chatting with a few friends who might be able to help turn my idea into a fully functional website. The friend who was crazy enough to talk to me more about the project was Zack Gilbert (hello, Zack!). Zack liked the idea, but even more than just the idea, he liked the challenge. He asked me to write out a full feature list and would get back to me if the site was doable in the three-week timeline I approached him with. Just a few hours later he was on board and had already cobbled together a first working version of a web application I could log into and write in real-time for everyone to see (imagine you're watching someone typing in a Word or Google Doc).

At the same time I was convincing Zack to help me build the WatchMeWrite website, I was emailing a few companies I thought could be a good fit to sponsor the project. Luckily when you bring ideas to people you have an existing relationship with, the ask is easier. But the ask is even easier when you have weird ideas they haven't seen before. My hope with having paying sponsors was that I could cover all the costs that go into self-publishing a book (editor, copyeditor, book formatter, etc.).

I knew I didn't want more than two sponsors for the project, so I kept my outreach low and included sentences in my emails like "I'm being totally honest here. You're one of three people I'm emailing about this." In my email to the first sponsor that hopped onboard, Acuity Scheduling, I owned my weird and wrote the line: "Okay, Gavin. Hold onto your butts!" You're welcome for teaching you how to write effective sponsor pitch emails!

After a few emails and Skype calls, Acuity Scheduling and Podia (formerly Coach) had officially come onboard as sponsors of a project that didn't have a website, didn't have official dates, and that I wasn't even sure could be built in the timeline that fit my schedule. They believed in the idea of WatchMeWrite, and most important, believed I could make it happen based on my track record.

I don't mean to shortchange all the hard work that Zack put into taking my initial designs for the WatchMeWrite website and turning them into a fully functioning entity, but let's be honest with each other: Zack knows Level 13 Developer Wizard magic and I can't share all his secrets.

In just three weeks, Zack made WatchMeWrite.co a reality, including the real-time writing application people could watch that would keep me free of distractions so I could simply focus on writing every day.

Over the course of fourteen days (yes, fourteen days, people!), I wrote just under eighty thousand words. I took one day off (to be a complete slob and watch NFL RedZone for eight hours) and spent half the time writing from a "writing cabin" in the desert in Joshua Tree. From 9 a.m. to 1 p.m. (PST) starting on December 1, I wrote the words and sentences for this book live for anyone to see. People from around the world visited the WatchMeWrite website. Google Analytics tells me that people watched from Japan, Israel, South Korea, Canada, Brazil, Argentina, Italy, Nigeria, South Africa, New Zealand, and tons of other countries. (Sadly, no one from Greenland stopped by. Ugh, next time!)

The first few days were the weirdest. Letting people see how bad the first draft of a book is was truly humbling. The final version of a book has gone through all the shiny filters and editorial stages. But the first version? Everyone got to see all my typos, grammar mistakes, and moments where all I could think was: "what the heck do I write next?"

But like anything else in life, as I continued to log in daily and write, it became more natural. My writing environment (the editor that Zack built) featured almost nothing. A simple toolbar and a column of white space for typing. I kept another browser tab open with the live site, but only allowed myself to check back in once or twice the first few days. When I got closer to the finish line of the first draft, I could more easily bounce from writing a thought to asking live viewers a question in the chat box that they hung out in daily.

One of my favorite parts of the WatchMeWrite project was the immediate feedback loop. If I got stuck down a certain line of thinking and couldn't figure my way out I'd pop over to the live chat and ask folks what they would want to know next. Within seconds I'd have questions from actual humans who cared about the words I was writing. That live interaction became my immediate cure for any inkling of writer's block.

After each day's writing hours ended, the WatchMeWrite website would essentially close down. If you wanted to read the previous writing entry I had just finished, you could donate a couple bucks. Otherwise, you'd have to wait a few hours for me to write again on the next day, or just wait for this book to become a finished thing. Also after each day's writing ended, I would flip on a microphone and record some thoughts for a daily audio journal/podcast. This was just as much an outlet for me as it was for other people to hear the behind the scenes of what it felt like to write a book, and especially to write a book live. I missed a couple days of recording podcast episodes about WatchMeWrite, and it had everything to do with making sacrifices (as I've talked about in this book). You can't go back and read the initial writing entries for this book, but you can open iTunes (or your podcast player of choice) and search "WatchMeWrite" to listen back to those daily audio recordings.

From all angles, WatchMeWrite was successful. This isn't the case with all my projects, as you've read, but this one came together just right. It was an awesome accountability partner that motivated me every day to sit in the chair and type the words that would become this book. It was a unique idea that attracted paying sponsors who helped make publicly writing the first draft of this book a profitable risk (hurray for that!). It also helped inspire other people to work on projects and ideas of their own. It was a completely different way to write a book and build a little marketing buzz in the process.

Someone asked me on Twitter: "Why would you risk writing your book live for everyone to see?"

My answer to them then and now is: "Because it felt different and felt like something that would motivate me and inspire other people."

And I hope it has inspired you.

Acknowledgments

THIS BOOK MADE POSSIBLE BY . . .

There are two companies that believed in me and gave me money to write this book. They didn't know anything about Own Your Weird, they simply believed in my crazy ideas and antics.

podia

Thank you to Spencer Fry from Podia (previously Coach). I'd actually never met Spencer before one of his colleagues (hey David!) reached out and introduced Podia to me. One thing led to another and I managed to get Spencer to sponsor the WatchMeWrite project of this book. If you're an entrepreneur who wants to sell digital products, I highly suggest you set this book down (only for a minute!) and go to podia.com. Spencer and his team have created a fantastic one-stop shop for online business owners and it may save you hours of time and heaps of money paying for separate business services. Thanks again, Spencer!

Thank you also to Gavin Zuchlinski from Acuity Scheduling. Gavin was a listener of a podcast I co-host (Invisible Office Hours) and emailed in asking to sponsor our show. One sponsorship led to another, and I also swindled Gavin into giving me money. Man, I should write a book about that . . . or is this that book? I love the story behind Acuity Scheduling, but I also really enjoy their calendar scheduling product that I use all the time to schedule calls with other people. If you hate time zones and calendar scheduling, go to acuityscheduling.com and jump in their free trial immediately. Thanks for the ongoing support Gavin, and congrats on the little Zuchlinski!

THANK YOU . . .

Thank you to my amazing wife who has fully embraced all my weirdness for nearly a decade. I can't imagine being on the other end of some of the ideas that spew from my brain, but she does it with support, love, and enough thoughtful criticism to bring out the best in me and my ideas. Caroline, you are an amazingly creative, emotionally in-tune, beautiful, and intelligent person with whom I love sharing this thing called life. You truly do bring out the best in me and I like to think I keep you on your toes (c'mon, wouldn't life be boring without me?). I can't thank you enough for your help with this book but also for opting in on our marry-ment and the many weird adventures we've been on and will continue to go on. I love you. (Look at that, it's written in print!)

Thank you to my family for always supporting my out-of-the-box ideas. I understand it must have been interesting seeing me grow from a curious kid to a question-everything adult. While I know my erratic life changes didn't always jibe with what you wanted for your lives, you supported me, trusted me, and loved me all the same. I fully understand that I'm a difficult person to be around at times because of how I see the world, but you never make me feel like an outsider in our family. (It's just the truth! Haha.) Oh, and Grama, keep signing up for all the new apps and social networks, it's the highlight of my day when I get to tell people my Grama is on Twitter and Instagram!

Thank you to our Wandering Aimfully community. Back in 2015 I almost didn't have the community part of BuyMyFuture, but that part has morphed into one of the things I look forward to most every day of my life (besides my pour-over coffee and vegan donuts, obviously). You creative weirdos are such an amazing group of people who have raised your hands for Caroline and myself many times over. You believe in the work we do, the messages we put out, and I hope you understand just how much each and every one of you WAIMers mean to me/us. That's not hyperbole, it's Jason-Zook-real-talk (and you know that carries weight!). We love your faces, keep owning your weird!

Thank you to the group of talented folks in the writing world who made this book's (weird) journey possible. Leila Campoli, I'm so glad my DearBookPublisher project was put in front of you and I love how much you embraced my weirdness! You're a pro at what you do, but, more important, you're helpful, honest, and someone I'd trust with any of my ideas. I hope this book's journey is one of many for us! Jennifer Kasius, thanks for pushing me to make this book as unique and helpful as possible. For asking all the right questions throughout the stories in the chapters in this book to make it as fun, impactful, and helpful for the folks reading it. I imagine you had to embrace some of your own weird when you stepped up to the plate to work on this book and I'm grateful you did! Lizzie Vance, you're a true unicorn and I couldn't have done the WatchMeWrite project or have finished the first draft of this book without you. It's fun to think back where we started together with my writing and I'm amazed that you wanted to help me given how cringeworthy my written work was in 2013! You're a saint and a talented human. And last but not least in the writing department of thank-yous: the folks at Running Press whom I never talked to but who said "YES" to a weird guy who bucks convention at every turn and simply wants to help other people do the same. Thank you for helping me spread my message further than I could spread it on my own.

And of course, thank YOU dear reader. I know I speak for many other authors when I say how much it truly means to know you took the time to pick up this book and read it. It's not easy writing a book, but knowing people pick up and read your work keeps us authors going! My hope is that you walked away feeling empowered, excited, and willing to embrace your weirdness quite a bit more in life and business. You can probably tell by now, but I'm 100 percent down for your honest feedback and to hear if this book motivated and helped you in some way. Feel free to email me or connect with me on social media. I'd love to hear from you and I'd especially love to know how you're owning your weird!

Index